Muhammad

A Story of the Last Prophet

Deepak Chopra

HARPER LUXE

An Imprint of HarperCollins*Publishers*

HarperCollins books may be purchased for educational, business, or sales promotional use. For information please write: Special Markets Department, HarperCollins Publishers, 10 East 53rd Street, New York, NY 10022.

FIRST HARPERLUXE EDITION

HarperLuxe™ is a trademark of HarperCollins Publishers

Library of Congress Cataloging-in-Publication Data is available upon request.

ISBN: 978-0-06-200251-8

10 11 12 13 14   ID/RRD   10 9 8 7 6 5 4 3 2 1

Contents

Author's Note

A great surprise awaited me when I began writing the story of Muhammad, the last prophet to emerge from the Middle Eastern desert—the endless, bleak, arid land that produced Moses and Jesus. Muhammad has suffered under centuries of disapproval outside the Muslim world. Ours is not the first age to react suspiciously when told by adherents that "Islam" means "peace." That suspicion only turns darker when extremist *jihadis* become terrorists in Muhammad's name.

In his own lifetime, the Prophet fought strenuously against his opponents and led armies into battle for the new faith. I grew up in India among Muslim friends, but even there, where mingled cultures and religions are an ancient way of life, the partition of Pakistan in

1945 led to riots and mass murder on both sides. In the name of truth, believers can easily trample love and peace.

None of that came as a surprise, however. I was determined to be fair to Muhammad and see him as he saw himself in seventh-century Arabia—we can locate his birth in 570 CE, in the middle of Europe's Dark Ages, two centuries before Charlemagne was crowned emperor by the pope in 800, almost six hundred years before the spires of Chartres cathedral first pointed heavenward in the twelfth century. That's where the surprise occurred, because among all the founders of the great world religions, Muhammad is the most like us.

Muhammad saw himself as an ordinary man. His relatives and neighbors didn't part and make way when he walked down the parched dirt streets of Mecca. He was orphaned by the age of six, but otherwise nothing exceptional stands out other than his ability to survive. Because he existed in a fiercely tribal society, Muhammad had numerous cousins and other males of the Hashim clan surrounding him as his extended family. There was no mark of divinity on him (except those invented by later chroniclers as Islam prospered and spread). He grew up to be a merchant who happened to marry well, taking a rich widow, Khadijah, as his wife, even though she was fifteen years his senior. He traveled in caravans to Syria one season and Yemen the next. Mecca owed its prosperity to the caravan trade. Even though these sojourns were beset with danger—Muhammad's handsome, favored father, Abdullah, had died on his way home from one trip—merchants of Muhammad's class routinely made journeys across the desert that lasted several months at a time.

What is extraordinary is that there are so many marks of common humanity in Muhammad's transformation. Jesus is being exalted when he is called the Son of Man; Muhammad deliberately blends in when he calls himself "a man among men." He could neither read nor write, but that was common enough, even among the well-to-do. He had four daughters who survived birth and two sons who died in infancy. Doing without an heir was unthinkable, and so he took the unusual step of adopting a freed slave boy, Zayd, as his son. Otherwise, it is inexplicable that God should reach down into a settled husband and father's life to speak through him. The most remarkable fact about Muhammad is that he was so much like us, until destiny provided one of the greatest shocks in history.

In the year 610 CE, Muhammad, a forty-year-old businessman known as Al-Amin, "the trustworthy," marched down from the mountains—or in this case a cave in the semiverdant hills surrounding Mecca—looking shattered and frightened. After literally hiding under the covers to regain his wits, he gathered the few people he could trust and announced something unbelievable. An angel had visited him in the cave, where Muhammad regularly went to escape the corruption and distress of Mecca. He sought peace and solitude, but both were destroyed when Gabriel, the same archangel who visited Mary and guarded Eden with a flaming sword after God banished Adam and Eve, abruptly ordered Muhammad to "recite."

The precise word is important, because "to recite" is the root word of Koran (or Qur'an). Muhammad was thunderstruck at this angelic command. He wasn't someone who joined in the practice of public recitation, for which the Bedouin were famous. As a boy he had been sent to live with nomadic tribes in the desert, a common practice among prosperous Meccans. It was felt that the purity and hardship of desert life was good for a child. At the very least it took him away from the foul air and depraved city ways of Mecca. Among the Arabs the Bedouin were considered to speak the purest Arabic, but for the rest of his life Muhammad would betray his sojourn among the nomads, which lasted from his birth to the age of five, by having a rustic accent. The Bedouin were also famous as storytellers.

They recited long legendary tales in praise of tribal heroes who conducted daring raids to seize camels and women from their warring neighbors. But Muhammad sat on the periphery as a listener rather than a participant, and he remained mute, so far as history is concerned, up to the moment when Gabriel found him.

The angel couldn't persuade Muhammad easily. He had to lock him in a tight embrace three times—a mythical, mystical number—before he agreed to recite. What came out of the Prophet's mouth were not his own words. To him and to those who began to believe his message, the fact that Muhammad had never recited in public proved that his words came from Allah. To this day, the Arabic in which the Koran is couched is singular, creating its own style and expressive world. Outside Islam, the only suitable comparison is probably the King James Bible, whose language resonates with English speakers as if spoken by either God or a chosen one who had been gifted with a divine level of utterance.

Because Muhammad never expected to be divinely inspired, the more tragic our suspicion and fear of Islam today. The pre-Islamic world feels much farther away than even the world of the Old Testament. Slaves were kept and cruelly abused. So were women, and unwanted baby girls were routinely left to die on a mountainside after they were born. Arabs used knives to settle even petty arguments, and they thought it honorable to murder men from neighboring tribes. Revenge was something to be proud of.

None of these ways, barbaric as they are, belong to Arabs alone. All can be found in various other early cultures. But Islam has been branded with barbarity in a unique way, in part because, in its zeal to maintain the Prophet's world as well as his word, the customs of antiquity have been preserved into modern times. I portray Mecca as it really was, which means in all its harshness and brutality. To lessen the impact of our modern-day judgments, I use multiple narrators to share in telling the story. My storytellers are women and men of every caste, slaves and rich merchants, believers and skeptics, idol worshipers and eager followers of Muhammad's message alike. The first people to hear the Koran had as many reactions to it as you or I would if our best friend collared us with a tale about a midnight visit from an archangel.

I didn't write this book to make Muhammad more holy. I wrote it to show that holiness was just as confusing, terrifying, and exalting in the seventh century as it would be today.

After that, the other issues were fairly minor. Ornate Arab names can be difficult for outsiders to remember, so I have minimized the number of characters in the book, keeping it down to the most important. Spelling is doubly confusing, since the same words and names are transcribed several ways. I haven't been consistent here. At the risk of irritating scholars, I've used the old, common spelling of "Koran." I've reduced long tribal names to easily remembered ones like Abu Talib and Waraqah. And since the hamza (') and 'ayn ('), for example, in a word like "Ka'aba," have no significance in English, I've done away with most of them, again in keeping with old, common usage. If sophisticated Arabic speakers are offended, I apologize in advance.

Finally, this is a novel, not an official biography. A few events are told out of order. Characters drop in and out of sight as needed to keep the tale going. This could lead to confusion. To help orient readers, I have provided a chronology of the most prominent events in the story. It is followed by a simplified family tree showing Muhammad's ancestry and extended family. The people who appear as characters in this novel are printed in boldface, for ease of recognition.

An author has no business coaxing his readers into how they should respond. I can tell you, however, that what drew me to this story was my fascination with the way in which consciousness rises to the level of the divine. This phenomenon links Buddha, Jesus, and

Muhammad. Higher consciousness is universal. It is held out as the ultimate goal of life on earth. Without guides who reached higher consciousness, the world would be bereft of its greatest visionaries—fatally bereft, in fact. Muhammad sensed this aching gap in the world around him. He appeals to me most because he remade the world by going inward. That's the kind of achievement only available on the spiritual path. In the light of what the Prophet achieved, he raises my hopes that all of us who lead everyday lives can be touched by the divine. The Koran deserves its place as a song of the soul, to be celebrated wherever the soul matters.

Chronology

(Because of the lack of verified dates, the ones listed below are approximate.)

570 CE	Birth of Muhammad
590	Muhammad's marriage to Khadijah, which produces four daughters, and two sons who die in infancy
610 (or earlier)	Muhammad's first revelation
613	First public preaching
615	Immigration of some Muslims to Abyssinia
616–619	Muhammad's clan, the Banu Hashim, boycotted by the Quraysh tribe

619	Deaths of Khadijah and Abu Talib
622	Hijra (migration) to Medina
624	Battle of Badr, Muslim victory against larger Qurayshi forces; Jewish tribes expelled from Medina
625	Battle of Uhud, a victory for the Quraysh that is not followed up on
627	Medina besieged by Meccan army (Battle of the Trench); Qurayza Jews of Medina massacred
628	Treaty of Hudaybiyah, calling a truce with the Quraysh
629	Peaceful pilgrimage to Mecca
630	Mecca occupied by Muslims; tribal enemies defeated in other campaigns
631	Islam accepted in many parts of Arabia
632	Death of Muhammad

MUHAMMAD:
A GENEALOGY

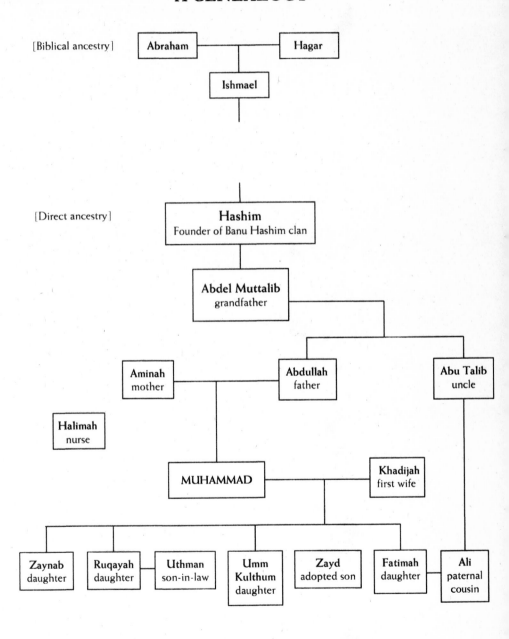

[Biblical ancestry]

Abraham — Hagar

Ishmael

[Direct ancestry]

Hashim
Founder of Banu Hashim clan

Abdel Muttalib
grandfather

Aminah
mother

Abdullah
father

Abu Talib
uncle

Halimah
nurse

MUHAMMAD

Khadijah
first wife

Zaynab
daughter

Ruqayah
daughter

Uthman
son-in-law

Umm Kulthum
daughter

Zayd
adopted son

Fatimah
daughter

Ali
paternal cousin

Muhammad

Prelude
The Angel of Revelation

A mule can go to Mecca, but that doesn't make him a pilgrim.

God didn't put those words in my mouth. He could have; he has a sense of humor. Those are Arabs' words. They are a people of many words, a flood that could float Noah's ark. If you're a stranger, you might not see that. You'd be blinded by the desert sun that bleaches bones and minds alike.

The sun takes on other tasks. Drying up water holes that ran full just last year. Starving the whole crop of spring lambs when the grass became parched and withered. Driving nomads in desperation to seek better pastures. And when they got there, the sun glistened off fresh blood, because other tribes who would die without their pastures lay in wait to kill the nomads.

But the Arabs refuse to give up. "Let's turn it all into a story," they said. "The cure for misery is a song." There are other cures, but no one had the money to buy them.

And so they set out to turn starvation into a heroic adventure. Thirst became a muse, the threat of murder a cause to boast of their bravery. Arabs and God had in common this love of words. So when He heard a man say, in the depth of his heart, "God loves every people on earth but the Arabs," it was fitting that I should appear with one command.

"*Recite!*"

That's all that I, Gabriel, was sent to say. One word, one messenger, one message. I was like a hammer knocking the bung out of a wine cask. One stroke, and wine to fill a hundred jugs spills out.

And so they did from Muhammad, but not at first. If an angel could doubt, I would have. I spoke to the one man in Arabia who didn't know how to recite. He sang no songs, much less an epic. He sat on the edge of the crowd when a wandering poet lifted his voice. Can you believe it? Muhammad had begged for God to speak to him, and when God answered, he was struck dumb.

Recite! What's wrong with you? Be filled with joy. The day that was heralded is now at hand.

Not him.

When I appeared, I found Muhammad in a cave on the side of a mountain.

"What makes you go there?" his friends demanded. "A merchant of Mecca should be tending his business."

Muhammad replied that he went up there for solace.

"Solace from what?" they asked. "You think your life is any harder than ours?"

They saw only a man in a purple-trimmed robe walking through the marketplace and sitting in the inns to make trades over tea. They never saw the man with shadows in his mind. Dark thoughts hid behind a smile.

One day Muhammad came home pale as a ghost. His wife, Khadijah, thought she would have to catch him in her arms if he fell.

"Do not go into the street," Muhammad ordered. He was actually trembling.

Khadijah rushed to the window, but all she saw in the street was a maid gathering bundles to carry away. The girl was crouched in the dust packing old rags, scraps of leather, and heaps of charcoal, tying them into bundles to sell in the hill towns around Mecca.

"Come away," Muhammad exclaimed, but it was too late. Khadijah saw what he had seen.

One of the bundles moved.

She closed the shutters with tears in her eyes. It could have been a cat that needed drowning. But Khadijah knew it wasn't. It was one more baby girl who would not grow up. One more forgotten corpse, small enough to hold in your hand, that no one would find on a remote hillside.

Muhammad was forty, and he had seen this abomination all his life. And worse. Slaves beaten to death on a whim. Rival tribesmen bleeding in the gutter, because they spat on someone's slipper. He did business with men who actually committed such acts and who shook their heads when Muhammad spoke of how much he loved his four daughters. Muhammad smiled at his friends and their fine grown sons. Only in his heart did he ask God why his two sons had died in the cradle. Only in his heart did he say the one thing that made a difference.

I will not turn my face from you, Lord, even if you kill everyone I love.

God could have whispered in return, "Why believe in me, if you also blame me for these evils?"

Perhaps he did whisper such a thought. Or Muhammad might have stumbled upon it on his own. He had time to think, in those long days and nights in a tiny mountain cave. He ate little, drank less. His wife worried that he might not come home again, since bandits infested the hills outside Mecca.

She was almost right. When I appeared before Muhammad, he would not recite the word of God, he would not listen, and he wouldn't even stay put.

Instead he fled the cave, running up the mountain in a frenzy of alarm. The man who wished for God to notice him was terrified once he was noticed. Muhammad stole a glance over his shoulder. The ground was rocky, and he stumbled. The air was filled with strange sounds. Did he hear the mockery of demons following him? Muhammad looked at the sky for answers. He wanted a way out.

He remembered the cliffs at the summit of Mount Hira. Shepherd boys had to be careful to keep lambs from running too close to the edge when a vulture circled overhead and frightened them.

What is circling me now? Muhammad thought with a surge of dread.

With a squeezing pressure in his chest, Muhammad gasped as he ran. He would jump from the cliffs and dash his body against the rocks below. He couldn't even pray for rescue, since the same God who might save him was the God who was torturing him.

I didn't ask for this. Let me go. I am nothing, a man among men.

Panting and stumbling, Muhammad clutched his robe tight against the gathering chill of Ramadan, the ninth month of the calendar. An evil month, a blessed month, a month of omens and signs. Arabs had argued over it as long as he could remember. After a few minutes the glaze of panic decreased. His mind was suddenly very clear. Muhammad looked down at his feet pounding over the ground as if they belonged to someone else. How curious—he had lost a sandal but didn't feel the jagged stones that cut his foot and caused it to stream blood. The decision to commit suicide brought a kind of comfort.

Muhammad gained the summit of the mountain. He spied Mecca in the distance. Why had he pursued God like a falcon after a desert hare? Mecca had hundreds of gods already. They lined the Kaaba, the sacred place, inside and out. One god for every worshiper; one idol for every sacrifice. What right did he have to meddle? There were countless sacrifices, day after day, that lined the town's pockets. Muhammad could almost smell the smoke from this great height.

Peering down at the rocks below, he trembled. In that moment of his destruction, Muhammad found a prayer that might save him.

Dear God, in your infinite mercy, make me who I was before. Make me ordinary again.

It was the one prayer God could not grant, for in that moment a man's existence was shattered like a wine cup carelessly trampled in a tavern. He would never be ordinary again. The only thing that mattered from now on would be Muhammad's words. The Arabs, as lovers of words, were poised. Would they love God's messenger or revile him?

Muhammad smiled faintly. A Bedouin saying had come to him: "A thousand curses never tore a shirt." *So why should I tear it myself? And my flesh and bones with it?* he thought. The image of his body crumpled and broken on the rocks below repelled him.

Muhammad turned away from the brink. *If I'm your vessel, handle me with care. Balance me lightly. Don't let me crack.*

I whispered yes. Who was I to deny him? I didn't even ask God first.

The merchant of Mecca limped with one sandal back down the slope. His tongue was thick and clumsy. Muhammad would recite as I commanded. He would never stop reciting, even if it meant his death.

ONE

The Water of Life

1.

Abdul Muttalib, "the Slave"

C an God's love be so intense that it feels like hate?" I asked.

"Don't speak of God," my son grumbled. "He isn't thinking about us right now."

We were dragging a sledge loaded with water jugs to town. The water, which was brackish and warm, sloshed out whenever we struck rocky ground.

"God thinks about everything, and he does it all at once. That's what makes him God," I replied mildly. I looked over at my son, Abdullah, who was yoked to the sledge with a band of rope around his bare chest. It was backbreaking work, and he was in a temper.

We had drawn the worst lot when the water carriers gathered at dawn. Forty young men were sent by the tribes every morning to bring water into Mecca.

There were no wells in town, and so water had to be hauled from the small wells that lay on the outskirts. Abdullah and I drew the farthest one, more than a mile away. Yoked like animals, bent low enough to eat the dust beneath our feet, we would be dragging the sledge until after sundown.

No one had pity for me, the old man. They all knew me as "the Slave," and the name made them treat me with veiled contempt.

"I used to think God hated me," I said, ignoring Abdullah's sour temper. "My childhood was full of poverty and woe."

"It's a curse to be here now."

I stopped pulling and spread out my arms. "I am in Mecca, my son, delivered into her holy gates by a miracle. What feels like hatred must be God's love in disguise."

Abdullah grunted. He had no interest in his father's foolish miracle. All he cared about was being awakened out of a heavy sleep to walk through the predawn darkness. He had half a mind to rebel. He was the youngest son of ten, favored and handsome. His noble nose was so large that it touched the wine before his lips did. More than anything, though, he hated that his father, a rich man, bore the nickname "the Slave."

"If I have to listen to you," Abdullah said petulantly, "let me walk in the shade." Water carriers stayed in the shade of houses and walls as much as they could, but now there was only a sliver of cool darkness, just enough for one man to creep into.

"You get the shade on the way back. We tossed for it."

"On the way back the jugs are empty. It's not fair."

I shrugged and leaned into my harness. The sun was at its highest point. The heat burned my skin like a stove.

Love that feels like hate. That riddle had been on my mind for days. To me it was the whole mystery of life, only I hadn't seen it before. Every curse is a blessing in disguise. Take this land of Arabia. Like a dangling jewel, it lies in the grasp of two empires. To the north the Byzantines hold out their fist, to the east the Persians. Surely that was a curse for a defenseless, scattered people like us. Yet the Arabs have never been conquered. The desert is too vast, too bleak. Wander off the trail for barely an hour, into the wasteland where only *jinns* and scorpions thrive, and you would be lucky to find your way back alive.

Even there God has shown his mercy, because traders couldn't sail around Arabia, not with pirates waiting in every cove and harbor. They were forced to march their precious silk and spices across the desert to Damascus. The result was prosperity for any town like

Mecca lucky enough to be on their route. The tribes praised the gods and vowed to make sure every traveler had water when he entered the city. Which only led to the next curse, that the water had to be hauled in every day, no matter how many backs it broke.

On and on life goes, like a necklace where one bead is a pearl and the next one poison.

No one wants to hear me babble about it. It was only the noonday sun that made me open my mind to my petulant son. Two nights ago, my obsessions with God's love became inescapable, and I lay awake with anxiety like a cold fever. I had taken a drastic, foolish step that day. I confessed to my cousins over a bout of wine drinking. It was at one of the tiny inns that cater to pilgrims near the Kaaba, where local men also meet.

"I cannot find a single blessing from God that is not also a curse," I said. "And no curse that is not also a blessing. Why is this so?"

There was silence. What was I talking about? My cousins only discuss three things: money, women, and camels.

One of them spoke up. "I lost another camel yesterday. Either my slave is faking the numbers, or he is letting raiding parties in for a pretty penny."

"If he was paid off, they'd take more than one camel," observed another cousin.

"Perhaps," the first cousin replied.

But I wouldn't be put off. "You don't care if God has cursed us? God has spoken to every people but the Arabs. Are we lost children who will never find our father's home again?"

The company went silent again. It made them nervous to hear me say "God" instead of "the gods." "It is so because it is so," remarked the oldest cousin, who gets exceptionally drunk every day and is exceptionally respected. The others nodded, and the conversation ended there.

I didn't expect an argument. The inn falls under the shadow of the Kaaba. All the ground around that sacred place is a sanctuary. No tribal fighting can break out there; blood feuds were cancelled; even violent argument has been outlawed. And I am chief of his clan, after all, so my cousins give me respect by listening with serious faces, even though they laugh at me on the inside.

My confession had done me no good. I couldn't sleep any better. Try and understand. I wasn't having philosopher's insomnia. This mystery applied directly to me—it would determine if my whole family survived.

It all began with water, a long time ago, in the age when memory began. After the raging waters of the Flood receded, and Father Noah descended from the ark, he bred a holy line of offspring. From his blood came Abraham, and from Abraham his firstborn son, Ishmael.

Now Ishmael's mother, Hagar, had only been a slave out of Egypt, belonging to Abraham's wife, Sarah. Because she was barren, Sarah told Abraham to take Hagar as his second wife in order to have children. Fourteen years later, a miracle came to pass, and Sarah became with child. She bore a son named Isaac. Afterward she demanded that Hagar be driven with Ishmael into the wilderness. Abraham bowed his head and obeyed.

When Hagar was wandering with the young boy, she grew desperately thirsty. There was no shelter under the open sky and no water in sight. Searching for a few drops to moisten Ishmael's parched mouth, Hagar went back and forth between the two hills known as Safa and Marvah. Ishmael began to cry. She was on the point of fainting, and they both might have perished, but God took pity on Hagar. He sent down the angel Gabriel, who touched the ground with his finger. At that spot the earth grew dark with moisture, and then the faintest trickle of water appeared. A miracle! Hagar bent down and drank, first cupping her palm to scoop water up for the boy.

As it is related, either Hagar or the angel said, "More. Let the waters accumulate," which in Arabic caused the well to be named Zamzam, "the water that accumulates." Mecca grew up around it. As a sign of God's favor, Ishmael and his heirs had sole possession of the well and the right to sell the water for all time.

When I was a boy and first heard the story, I wouldn't have questioned a miracle. Couldn't I walk up to the Kaaba and touch its walls, where every stone is a miracle? Abraham had built it, the House of Allah, near where the well bubbled up. It was exactly like the first building that Adam had put up with his own hands, made of granite blocks and perfectly square on all sides. Arabs began to call it Kaaba. Through every tribal war and every invader's attempt to vanquish us, it remained the House of God, long after the well of Zamzam, once the perpetual spring, had disappeared, for even Zamzam had a curse upon it, although it was many generations before anyone found out.

I looked over at Abdullah, who had taken to muttering under his breath. He was twenty and brawny enough for hauling water, but this was his first time. He had begged me to tell him why we were doing this menial drudgery, not even allowing ourselves a donkey cart. But I would say only one word, "Later."

"Take my shade," I offered.

"Your shade? Is that what you call it?" Abdullah was as proud as a rich man's son ought to be.

Ignoring the rebuke, I pushed him into the shade of a high wall that circled a courtyard. Our own courtyard was the nearest to the Kaaba, a great mark of rank. Water had made me rich, but the seasoning to the feast was the envy others felt for me. I could taste it when I strolled to the marketplace every morning.

I said, "I've never told you about the miracle that brought me to Mecca. It's time you learned."

Abdullah didn't look surprised. I had made the same speech to each of my ten sons when they reached a certain age. "Your grandfather, Hashim, was the chief of our tribe. He preciously guarded the right to haul this water, which brought him revenue from every pilgrim and a tithe from all the other tribes in Mecca. As a boy I had no knowledge of this, because Hashim died mysteriously while taking a caravan to Egypt. My mother tied me up in a bundle and ran away, suddenly penniless and without friends. Hashim's brother had claimed his fortune. I, his oldest son, was pushed aside."

Abdullah didn't question these events. When a woman's husband dies, it is permitted for his brother to inherit his property if there are no grown sons.

"I grew up forsaken in a faraway town, creeping like a snake between heaven and earth. In the eyes of all Arabs I was an orphan. I was nothing. The lowest point in life is exactly when God bestows his miracles,"

I said. "Are you ready to hear mine? Without it, you wouldn't be here, handsome as you are."

Abdullah grimaced. I was enjoying the power my story had over him. I went on. "Some years passed. My uncle, Al-Muttalib, suddenly became horribly guilty. He had grown wealthy from Hashim's right to carry water, yet he had deprived Hashim's son of his share. Guilt wouldn't leave him alone; it was relentless. Therefore Al-Muttalib decided that this was a sign. Without a word to anyone, he rode away from Mecca, found me with my mother in exile, and lifted us from the dust. He promised to treat me like a second son. Two days later I rode before him as Al-Muttalib reentered Mecca. Yet people couldn't believe that this dirty boy who couldn't even sit up on a camel was anything but a new slave being brought home. On all sides they called me Muttalib's slave: Abdul Muttalib."

"And that is our shame," muttered Abdullah. He has always been quick to draw his dagger if another young male ridiculed his father's insulting nickname. Out of habit everyone had forgotten my real name, Shaybah, and dubbed me "the Slave."

With a grunt I leaned into my harness. I'm still strong. I'm not yet fifty. Yoked beside me, Abdullah had no choice but to keep up. For a while we silently dragged the sledge. And he didn't offer to surrender the shade.

"I have given you knowledge today. So please answer me now. Can God's love be so intense that it feels like hatred?" I asked.

My son knew to take the question seriously. "The answer doesn't lie with God. It lies with your own guilt."

"Explain."

"If you cheated on my mother, maybe she would find out, maybe she wouldn't. But in your guilt, you could feel her love as disguised poison. And if a man kills his brother, as Cain killed Abel, his guilt might make God's love feel like hate."

"A good reply," I said. "But I am welcome in my wife's bed without sin, and I've killed no one. I thought that being rich is a blessing, but I was a fool."

Abdullah regarded me in disbelief, but I didn't let him interrupt. "You think my riches aren't a curse? That's why I came today to the gathering place to draw lots. I wanted to see for myself what this backbreaking work is like. Look at me. After half a day I'm ready to drop in the dirt and perish. Do you see what that means?"

Abdullah had no idea what it meant, unless it was that his father perversely wanted to suffer.

I read his thoughts. "For one moment forget your vanity. Even if I don't die from this ordeal myself, many young men will. I've seen their bodies wither; they fall sick. Stronger clans will easily wipe us out, or we will die out on our own, before our time."

"What can we do, sir?" Abdullah asked, for the first time showing respect. Among us Arabs, nothing is more important than the tribe. Ours was the Quraysh, the largest and most powerful in Mecca, which means that its downfall is in the prayers of every other tribe. It was unbearable for Abdullah to think of his whole race being annihilated one day.

"Zamzam," I murmured. "That is what we will do."

"What?" My son knew the name—everyone in Mecca did—but it was as legendary as Eden. He hadn't wasted a moment thinking about the water of life, as the elders called it, still less what it meant to lose it.

I said, "I have to find the well again. Once I do, there will be endless water right in the heart of town. We Quraysh will no longer pay for our wealth with our lives. What do you think of that?"

Abdullah was tempted to think his father had gone mad. I could see that. But he didn't dare say so. "You are asking God for a second miracle," he replied cautiously. "Perhaps that's one too many."

I laughed. "I swear, if I am ever made chief of chiefs throughout Arabia, you will be my ambassador. Such smooth diplomacy. Wait until the women hear you."

At this Abdullah brightened. As the handsomest of my sons, he had attracted glances from the girls all his life. But this was the first time I'd spoken of letting him approach a woman. Marriage couldn't be far off.

We had talked so long that we were close to the cistern by now where the water was needed. This particular cistern was a shallow stone tank no more than eight feet across. When we arrived, two dozen women were waiting with clay water jugs on their hips. At the sight of the sledge, they let out the piercing warbled cry of tribal nomads.

"There you go. More women than you can handle," I said.

I felt so wrung out that I let my vain, disgruntled son empty the heavy jugs from the sledge. Most of the water went to the waiting women, leaving barely two or three inches in the cistern. A cluster of palm trees nearby would shade it enough so that the heat didn't steal everything. I liked this place. I admired the palms, which survived cannily on the drops spilled by water carriers and careless women running back to their families.

I rubbed my chest where the rope harness had left burn marks. "Zamzam," I muttered softly. Could I really find it again? The truth is, I didn't have the courage to mention my mad plan to my cousins, or even my wife. The men of our tribe would be justified in stripping away my fees. A lunatic has no business with sacred water rights.

Maybe God himself was against me. To everyone in Mecca, Zamzam had disappeared as divine punishment. One night, long before anyone living can remember, a righteous man became outraged by the greed and insolence of the rich and impious Meccans. No one knows his name. He furtively entered the Kaaba and stripped it of gold offerings and sacred idols. Even though Allah was God, the one and only, the tribes had forgotten him and lined the sacred place with their own gods, hundreds of them.

After throwing his loot into the well, the thief covered Zamzam over with earth, burying it from sight. He uttered a prayer that the well never be found by the unrighteous. God must have listened, because when the sun came up the next day, no one could remember where Zamzam was. The rich despaired; a few even repented. But they were lost. Mecca dwindled without its precious water. The sons of Ishmael departed. The place became desolate for centuries, until the Quraysh revived the town. They established the system of carrying water from the outlying brackish wells. They rebuilt Mecca, provided inns for pilgrims, and made the Kaaba a proper house of worship as before. All of which entitled them to be called the new sons of Ishmael.

"Can we go home now?" asked Abdullah. His eye was fixed on a pretty maid swaying her hips as she walked away.

"You won't catch her stinking the way you do," I said.

"If the only thing that stands between me and a wife is a bath, I have no worries," Abdullah replied, certain of what he was talking about.

We wended our way home, the old man limping, leaning on the young one's shoulder.

But even dead on my feet, I heard a sound. A faint rumble that could have been a muffled voice. Somewhere, Zamzam flowed deep in the earth and was waiting to be reborn.

God's will is done in circles. No mind of man can fathom His hidden design. So, do not mock my obsession with finding the sacred well again. If I ever release its waters and perhaps even take possession of the gold that the thief flung into it, will God reverse His judgment?

"I beseech the blessing hidden in the curse," I murmured.

"Just as long as I'm not cursed with another day like this," grumbled Abdullah.

"You'll go to your aunt's house tonight," I said. "Some young marriageable women will be there. Try to control yourself. We wed one at a time."

Abdullah bowed low, mumbling profuse thanks for the invitation. One visit to a house of women made him as pleased as stealing some spring lambs from a rival tribe out in the hills. He began to whistle a love song.

When we were about to round the corner to our house, I said, "I can make it the rest of the way alone. I've sent word that one of your third cousins should run here, to finish the day's water hauling with you."

Abdullah's smile froze.

2.

Bashira,
the Hermit

It's important to ignore the voices. When I first came
to this horrible place, I was afraid of going mad. But
soon I wanted to go mad with every fiber of my being.
The old monk was still alive then, and he heard voices.
He said they came from God, but he had lost his mind
years ago.

The old monk spent every waking moment writing.
At first I was in awe, because I can only write my name.
I was taught how by the elder brothers, so that I might
sign my contract with Christ, to be his servant for life.

"What are you writing?" I asked the old monk,
whose named was Celestius.

"The Bible," he replied.

He gave me an irritated look. Celestius rarely spoke.
The usual sound that came from his mouth was the

crunch of his teeth on the flatbread we ate at every meal. Our grinding stone leaves grit in the flour, and his teeth had worn down to stubs.

But I must explain about the Bible. There is no Bible. The length and breadth of Arabia has never seen such a precious object, or if it has, the pagans buried it in the sand or ate it when they got truly desperate—boiled vellum might retain some bit of lamb fat. I myself saw a Bible only once, when it was placed against my forehead in Damascus, the day I gave my life to Christ, our Lord.

Trying to hide my disbelief, I asked Celestius, "Where is this Bible you are copying?" He must have hidden it well. Our cave contained two straw pallets for sleeping and a clay pot for washing. All the cooking had to be done outdoors or the smoke would choke us.

Celestius assumed a crafty look. "Don't need a Bible," he said tapping the brown-spotted dome of his bald head. "In here." He smiled secretly, showing his upper row of stubs.

Well, crazy is as crazy does. If he wanted to copy the Bible out of his head, so be it. I asked him to read a Psalm to me.

"Haven't gotten there yet," he said. "They told me to start at the beginning." And that was the end of the discussion. As punishment for interrupting him, he refused to acknowledge me for a month, as if I were invisible like his Bible.

I used to hear the Psalms through the church windows when I was lost on the street in Damascus. They aren't all about the valley of death, although there were days I wanted to go there, starving days in the back alleys that smelled of raw sewage. Sewage has its uses if you don't want someone to find you.

I will lift up mine eyes unto the hills,
From whence cometh my help.
My help cometh from the Lord,
Who made heaven and earth.

The Psalmist must not have seen the hills of Bostra that circle our cave. There's no help from there.

Or so I thought.

One day Celestius seemed to take longer than usual to unfold his creaking limbs in the morning. I poked him but he didn't move or let out a grunt. He had died sometime after midnight prayers. From the way his arm lay outstretched in the direction of my pallet, I suppose he had wanted the last rites. A bit late on that one, my brother. I put him in the earth with a rough marker on his grave. He would keep a long time, what with the lack of rain. Eventually a caravan would pass by carrying a Christian, and then the body could be taken back to Damascus for a proper burial.

I didn't fear loneliness. Actually, it was good to be rid of him. I love my fellow man, as Christ commands me to, but toward the end Celestius was too mad to remember to dress or clean himself. I saw his bony behind once too often. After I buried the old monk, a trader from Tyre came by one day who could read, and I showed him a stack of pages from Celestius's "Bible." The trader laughed and said it was complete gibberish. No surprise. The only thing of interest was the last page. On it Celestius had written the same line over and over until his hand faltered and the letters turned to faint squiggles:

When the sun's face is hidden, God will bring his last prophet.

"Are you sure that's what it says?" I asked. Because he was my guest, the trader had no reason to lie. I will grant the pagans one thing—they hold hospitality sacred. I had invited him into my cave for food and drink—a proper meal, not just flatbread and grasshoppers. I sell religious trinkets to travelers (with a little work a goat's shinbone can be made to look very much like a saint's), and with the money I buy supplies from the caravans. Dates and figs, usually, but also honey, olives, hard cheese, and dried meat. Wine, of course, in clay jars sealed with pitch.

The trader assured me that he had read the line just as it was written, but to be certain he took the page outside, where the setting sun still imparted an amber glow to the hills. *When the sun's face is hidden, God will bring his last prophet.* Celestius wasn't sure about the spelling of the word "prophet," so he had put in three versions and one of them was right, the trader told me. The trader said he'd be glad to read the other gibberish to me too, but that just meant he wanted more wine. I gave him another cup out of charity, even though my heart sank inside. This man from Tyre had delivered me a world of trouble without knowing it.

God will bring his last prophet. Impossible. The old monk was simply delirious. God has already sent his only begotten Son. The prophecy of Isaiah is fulfilled. Unless . . .

Unless Jesus has forsaken us.

Unless God has changed His mind.

Unless the Devil has found me in the smallest, darkest, dirtiest cave on the face of the earth.

What a curse when the mind hits upon that tiny exception—*unless.* It appears like a black mote on the far horizon. And no matter how hard you struggle, the speck grows and grows until one day it swallows up the sky. What could I do? I prayed. I asked God for a sign. One night after thrashing in bed covered in sweat, I rose and burned all the pages the old monk had scribbled. Yet when I got to the last one, fear gripped my heart, and I couldn't put it to the flame. So either God or the Devil has power I couldn't resist.

After that I spent my days watching the sky, waiting for the face of the sun to be hidden. A stranger found me that way, squatting on the ground outside my cave.

"Why are you staring at the sun, old one?"

I looked up to see a tall, turbaned man who was as dark as his shadow. Perhaps an Abyssinian. They say that if you cross the sea to their kingdom, which is Christian by the grace of God, there are many Bibles, some covered in cloth of gold. Maybe here was a man I could talk to.

"I'm not staring at the sun," I replied.

"Good. The sun is the eye of Nabul," he said. "You'll go blind if you gaze into it."

Nabul is one of their countless idols in this forsaken place. The stranger was an unbeliever. I got to my feet, so that when I told him to go away, we'd be looking eye to eye. Then I saw something over his shoulder. A cloud had appeared in the sky out of nowhere. In this land where sand dunes roll like an endless sea and rain falls only to moisten the graves of those who hear the Last Trumpet, there was a cloud.

I pointed with my finger. "Is that your caravan, stranger?" Camels and wagons crawled in the distance.

"I travel ahead of it as a scout. Those are traders from Mecca, and not very rich ones, either," he replied.

I barely heard the words. The cloud, which was not large, cast its ragged shadow on the earth. From up above I could see it clearly. What amazed me was this: the cloud was directly over one wagon in the caravan, and as the camels lumbered along the trail, the cloud moved with them, always shading one particular wagon.

"Who rides in that cart?" I asked.

The black man shrugged. "It could be anyone," he said.Except the slaves and servants, who were forced to walk. I could see a straggling line of them keeping pace with the camels. I counted. It was a small caravan by the standards of the great ones from Yemen when an engorged ship from the East has unloaded its cargo of silk, iron, perfumes, and spices. I counted no more than two dozen camels and three donkeys.

"You look pale," remarked the stranger. The next thing I knew, I felt something cool and damp being pressed against my forehead. I opened my eyes and touched my face with trembling hands.

"Maybe you were gazing into Nabul's eye after all," said the man. "You fainted." He pressed the damp cloth to my forehead again, but I pushed him away.

"I have to see," I mumbled and staggered to the mouth of the cave. Thank God I had not been unconscious for long. The threadlike procession of the small caravan was still in sight down below. And yes, the cloud was poised directly over one wagon. I watched until they were out of sight. Nothing changed. The face of the sun had been hidden, and God was protecting someone with cool shade. The possibility was staggering. I had to find out who was in that wagon.

For the rest of the afternoon I paced restlessly trying to think it through. The Devil could be tempting me. I hadn't seen the stranger walk up my hill, and I hadn't seen him depart. He could have been Satan's minion, able to appear and disappear as he was bidden. But the man hadn't asked me to renounce God, and he didn't leave me lying in the sun to die when I fainted. The Adversary doesn't do good deeds. Then I realized that this logic was ridiculous. If the Devil had found me, I was lost already. He'd gnaw at my soul like a desert rat by tiny, maddening bites until he got what he wanted.

In the end I waved to a village boy passing by with three skinny goats and told him to invite the men of the caravan to my cave for supper. He nodded and ran off.

The people around here have a superstitious regard for me. I swept the cave and brought out my best provisions. A rare mood had come over me. I whistled while cracking open the best wine jars, soaking the dates in water to plump them up, and throwing out any fig that had been infested with maggots. This was going to be a kind of last supper. Either God's word was coming true, or my soul was about to be snatched by madness. One way or another, the end had come.

Folded up under my pallet was an embroidered cloak that signified who I was—not a filthy beggar with matted hair, but a priest. When they sent me into the desert, the Damascene fathers presented it to me. "Never forget who you are," the abbot said gravely. "And don't come home until this is your winding sheet."

I smiled to myself, wrapping the scarlet cloth around my narrow shoulders. Moths had chewed small holes in the wool, but the gold embroidery twinkled in the dimness of the cave. The cloak was still a fine thing. I sat in the midst of the feast I had spread out and waited for sundown. Once or twice I nodded off—the aftermath of my great excitement—until I heard men's voices coming up the hill.

"Bashira. Are you he?" the head man said when he got to the mouth of the cave. These Arabs are horrible unbelievers, but they speak formally when they come as guests.

I lit an oil lamp and held it close to my face. "Is there another cave waiting for you that is set with a feast?" I asked.

The glow from the lamp illuminated my scarlet robe, giving it what seemed like an inner light. The Arabs looked at each other doubtfully. They believe in all kinds of spirits, especially those who roam the desert after nightfall to suck humans dry of their souls. But the lead man didn't falter. Seeing the food and drink all around me, he stepped inside with a bow.

They sat in a circle and began to eat. None of them said a prayer or cared two beans that I did. A couple of them splashed the floor with wine as offerings to their idol. The name didn't matter. Idols were more plentiful than horses or cattle. If you climbed a tree to escape a prowling jackal, you could turn that into your god if you wanted to.

Being guests, the men didn't attack the food like ravenous beasts, but ate with dignity. I sat silently and watched. Which one was the prophet? It wasn't long before dignity grew thin. As the wine flowed, the talk grew louder and coarser. To them I wasn't a holy man, so they spoke freely of women in the streets and their many conquests. The hours wore on. Tongues wagged, then heads nodded. But I kept my gaze alert. *Which one?* The full moon had sent slanting light into the cave for the first hour, but it had long set under the stark, treeless horizon. I turned to the head man, who had seated himself on my right. He wasn't sober, but he was still coherent.

"Is there anyone here I should know in particular?"

He looked puzzled, and why not? I had no words for what I wanted to say. I tried again. "I am looking for someone favored by the gods," I said. "Does any of your clan have a mark upon him?"

"What?" He shook his head in confusion and asked for another cup of wine. I gave it to him and sank back into my gloomy thoughts. Not for the whole evening had I seen a sign of God's intentions. These were coarse, ordinary traders, drifters across the face of the desert. Someone was toying with me.

The men rose to leave, each helping the other to his feet. They staggered out into the night, which had grown dark and thick without the moon. Torches were lit, and the head man bowed to me. He was about to turn away when he said, "I have put some dates and figs in my bag without asking your permission. They're for my son. Forgive me."

I tried to keep my voice from trembling. I asked him why his son stayed away. I had explicitly invited every man of the caravan. He said that they had left behind no men. His son was still a boy. They'd left him behind to guard the animals and raise the alarm at the first sign of raiders.

"Send the boy to me," I said. "My Lord Christ bids me to offer food to every stranger tonight, without exception."

To his superstitious mind this was logic enough, not that he had any regard for the name of Christ. The head man gathered his homespun skirts about him and sat down on the ground after barking orders at one of the others. His men bowed and departed down the hill.

"Actually, I'm happy you called for Muhammad," he said. "I felt guilty leaving him alone when one of the slaves could have watched over everything."

I remarked that I'd never seen a boy on caravan. They were dangerous affairs, weren't they?

He sighed. "Just so. My tribe has suffered from death in faraway countries. Our caravans have been cursed. Especially one time." He was leading to a tale, but suddenly he stopped and looked away.

Half an hour later his man returned, apparently alone. But as he got closer, I saw the outline of a small boy walking behind him. The two approached, and with beating heart I looked at the boy's face. He barely glanced my way, bowing to his father.

"Abu Talib, I am here to serve you," the boy said gravely. He looked to be about twelve, short and compact. In the dim glow cast by the cooking fire I couldn't see his eyes. Only when he was told to greet his host did he turn to me, and then his eyes were cast down to the ground.

"Your father says you are called Muhammad."

It was a simple statement, but the boy hesitated before nodding his head.

"Who are your people?" I asked. Before he could answer, his father interfered. He jumped to his feet and pulled him close. "To you our people are nothing, so why question a boy?"

I looked surprised. "You act as if I might hurt your son. What is it?"

"He's precious to me. His mother died when he was just barely walking."

That wasn't the whole story. These Arabs can take any number of wives, according to their custom. I had a burning need to know about this boy, and so I asked God what to say before he was snatched away. There was only a moment left; the head man wasn't anxious to stay. Suddenly I saw the truth.

"He isn't your son," I said flatly "You've been lying. Why?" My voice was clear and strong. "I am asking you as a holy man. God has told me something important, but first I must know the truth."

The head man grew nervous. A strange thing about the Arabs is that they respect the name of God, despite all their idols. It's not something they freely talk about, but I've been told that they know there is only one God. There was a time when their worship was pure. They even look to Abraham as their father. But over time they fell into idolatry.

"I need the truth," I repeated. "Who are you, Abu Talib?"

"I am his uncle and head of the clan," Abu Talib admitted with reluctance. "My lie wasn't a sin. I am the boy's protector."

"So he's an orphan?"

Abu Talib nodded, and the boy drew closer to him, folding his small body into his uncle's robe. I knelt down. "Muhammad, a caravan is a dangerous venture, but you're safe here. Will you speak with me? I implore you. Your fate is important. Or do you know that already?"

I put my forehead to the ground, as if addressing a superior. That would frighten an ordinary boy or make him burst out laughing, but Muhammad straightened up.

"What I know is my concern, not yours," he said.

"No, boy," his uncle said sharply, then turned to me. "Forgive him. His father, Abdullah, was proud."

"My concerns are God's, and he takes no offense. Yet I still need to speak to you." I kept my words and my eyes fixed on the boy.

He pondered for a moment.

"Are you asking your gods to decide for you?" I asked.

I named Al-Uzza, one of their female idols—a bitch goddess they pray to for fertility—whose name I had once overheard.

The boy scowled.

"She isn't your favorite? She's beautiful and has large breasts," I pointed out.

"Mocking me will only make me run away," he replied. "I won't touch any idols or perform their rites."

"Why not?"

"If you're a holy man, you already know. There is no God but God."

My heart jumped in my chest, and I had to hold my arms tight around myself to keep from reaching out to this strange child. If only he stood closer to the fire, so I could see his eyes. They would tell me. Abu Talib was gazing proudly at his nephew.

"He is special," I said, and he nodded. His uncle had no idea. None of them did. Their caravan would be moving on before dawn. Whatever I had to say, it had to be at that moment. Boldness was the only way.

"I know about you, far more than you imagine," I said. I put my hand on his shoulder and pulled him away from his uncle. Abu Talib could have taken serious offense, but he didn't move. I led Muhammad to a bowl-shaped depression in the ground. It was as far around as a man could stretch out and three hands deep.

"Can you guess who dug that hole? A crazy man. He was living in this cave before I came here. If I hadn't dragged him away, he would have clawed at the earth until his hands bled. He died one night without recovering his wits." I wasn't lying. Toward the end Celestius had forsaken the Bible and became obsessed with digging where his voices told him to. I tried to coax him out of his mad fixation, but he still managed to dig a sizable hole.

The boy's eyes widened with curiosity. "Why?"

"He thought the water of life was down there, and he had to find it."

Muhammad pointed to the jugs of water lined up at the mouth of the cave. "You mean them?"

I shook my head. "No, the villagers haul that up to me. The water of life doesn't flow out of the ground. It flows from here." I lightly touched his chest over the breastbone. "You were born in the desert, but it's a fearful place for me and every holy man. We come here for only one reason, to find the water of life."

"And did you find it?" he asked solemnly.

"Not for many, many years. The old monk who scratched at the earth had lost his mind. He despaired of ever finding it. But tonight my quest may be over."

Muhammad listened calmly, as if this all made perfect sense to him. His uncle was now visibly agitated. Unable to keep quiet, he burst in. "My family found it. The well was buried for centuries. But a dream came to my father, Abdul. He saw the very spot where Zamzam lay under the ground. He was our savior, blessed be his name."

In an excited voice he unfolded the tale, and even with a mongrel blend of Greek and Arabic, the tongues of traders, I understood. This well they call Zamzam was promised to them by God at the time of their ancestors, and it was to flow as long as time. But God became angry when the people turned to idol worship, and he made the well disappear. Mecca could have been a great city glorifying his name. Instead, God granted it only enough water to survive, and that had to be obtained by hard labor.

Abu Talib's father, "the Slave" as he was known, became obsessed with finding Zamzam. Some say he secretly swore an oath to sacrifice one of his sons if the gods showed him where to dig. Others say that he converted back to the one God of their ancestors. Whichever it was, Abdul was given a dream. He saw a spot between two of the largest idols, near to their house of pagan worship, the Kaaba. Everyone in his tribe laughed at him, but the Slave insisted on digging everywhere around that spot. Lo and behold, one day a man thrust his spade into the ground and hit something hard. It was a well cover, and when they removed it, water came forth. Zamzam had been found again, along with the golden hoard and idols that had been stolen from the Kaaba. Abdul returned them, keeping only a portion of the booty for himself.

Abu Talib stuck out his chest as he finished his tale. "So you see, my people have found the water of life. God showed it to us."

"God's works are mysterious," I said mildly.

His eyes narrowed. "You don't believe me?"

I had a polite answer on my tongue, but the boy Muhammad spoke up. "The well was a sign, sir. There is water no one can see, that never wets anyone's lips. That's what the holy man means."

The uncle looked confused, torn between anger at being called a liar and pride in his precocious nephew.

"Not just a sign," I said hurriedly. "A great sign. God has showered blessings on your tribe."

You'd think the uncle would have been pleased to hear this; after all, he had just said the same thing.

Instead, his face darkened. "My father, Abdul, used to swear that God's love is hard to tell from his hate. His favorite son, my brother Abdullah, died from a sudden sickness while coming home with a caravan. When we heard about it, messengers and physicians were rushed to him, but he had already been buried, no more than two days journey from his wife. They had been married only two months. She perished from grief, and now, but two years ago, my father followed them. If you really are a holy man, find the blessing in that."

The blessing is that you brought this boy to me.

Hiding my thoughts, I mumbled again that God's works are mysterious, and Abu Talib nodded sadly. This talk had unfolded many things close to his heart. Between that and the wine, he seemed to trust me, so I held tight to Muhammad's rough wool cloak and pulled him near the fire. He didn't object, and for the first time I could look into his eyes.

Ah.

"What do you see? Is he cursed too?" asked the uncle gloomily. "I took in my brother's son after he was orphaned. I've always tried to keep him safe."

"You haven't protected him well enough," I warned.

"No, don't say that! Only one good thing came from Abdul's dying. It broke his heart to lose Abdullah. He couldn't bear it if Muhammad will be snatched away too."

Abu Talib had misunderstood my meaning, but the boy didn't. He allowed me to keep gazing into his eyes. He was willing to let me see. Suddenly I couldn't keep back the tears. I began to weep silently, turning away so that the two of them might not notice.

"It's all right," Muhammad whispered. He laid his hand gently on my gray head, as if we had changed places and now I was the boy, he the man.

The uncle became even more alarmed at my behavior. "Tell me!" he cried.

There was no explaining my anguish. I felt my faith slip away from under me like sand under my feet. Where was my Lord? What would become of us poor seekers in the wilderness, waiting these long centuries?

I regained control and turned to Abu Talib.

"Pardon me. There is no curse. You must protect this boy as if he were your most precious possession. He is God's."

The uncle looked astonished, not just by my words, but by the calmness in Muhammad. "You still haven't told me what you saw."

"A light. Here." I put my finger lightly on the space between the boy's eyebrows.

I waited for the uncle to protest. Instead, he froze, and his head trembled. He turned to the boy. "Go." The word came out as a hoarse croak. He pointed toward the bottom of the hill, where the man who had brought Muhammad from camp was waiting in the dark to take him back.

Muhammad bowed without saying anything and left. When he was out of earshot, Abu Talib recovered the power of speech.

"There's a secret the boy doesn't know," he said. "He was born nine months to the day after Abdullah got married. My brother never saw him. Before he set out on the journey from which he never returned, Abdullah took me aside. He had a premonition, and he begged me to take care of his son. I was astonished, for no one knew that Aminah, his bride, had already conceived.

"Why come to me?" I asked. "There was our father, a wealthy man, to take care of his grandsons. And besides, of my father's ten sons, we all knew who his favorite was."

Abu Talib paused and waved his hand. "Never mind. It's all in God's hands. But Abdullah had a guilty conscience. That was his real reason for seeking me out in private. On his wedding day, he told me, he was walking to Aminah's house for the ceremony. My brother, being blessed with a handsome face, was used to women and their come-hither looks. And why not? He gave in more than once. On this day a married woman spied him from her window above the street. She became instantly enamored of this handsome groom and cried out for him to lie with her. My brother was no prude, but he was shocked. Her lustful call could be heard up and down the street. Even more shocking, she ran downstairs in her bare feet and approached him in the street, snatching at his scented robes. 'I must lie with you now, this very minute,' she pleaded. With difficulty Abdullah tore himself away, and an hour later he was married in Aminah's house, to great rejoicing.

"Men are only flesh. Even you, a holy man, must admit this, unless God has completely neutered you. That night Abdullah embraced his bride, but the next day at dawn he saw the face of the married woman. She was beautiful, and my brother felt a wave of lust overtake him. He fought it. He almost woke up his bride. Instead, he sneaked out of the house and ran back to the street where the married woman lived. The sun wasn't yet up. The cobblestones were cool under his feet. 'I must be crazy,' he thought. But he threw pebbles at the window shutters, and luckily for him, the woman heard instead of her husband. She stuck her head out and said, 'What do you want? Can't honest people sleep without the likes of you coming around, dog?' Abdullah was astonished at this change of behavior, and not a little offended. As I say, he was used to the attention of women. He threw a rock at her and demanded to know what had changed her mind. 'Yesterday when you came prancing down the street, you had a light between your eyes,' she said. 'It was as bright as a flame at midnight. I wanted that light for my child, but now you have slept with another, and her child has the blessing. Go away and leave me alone.'"

The uncle's agitation had hardly subsided as he recounted this story. "Abdullah never told that story to anyone but me. Is it true? Has the light been passed to Muhammad?"

There was no need for me to say anything, only to give the slightest nod. For some reason the pain in my heart had lessened. If God was bringing the last prophet, His will be done. It was left for me to pray and count my final days, which I am sure will be few. At least I was safe. The Devil hadn't been toying with me.

The uncle was anxious to get back to camp. He bowed to me and started down the trail. The horizon was just lighting up with the palest blue, not often seen by townspeople but every day by a hermit who rises to pray five times a night. I could make out the faint shape of Abu Talib's silhouette as he hurried down the stony path beyond the reach of the cooking fire, which had dwindled to embers.

Abu Talib would remember to take special care of the boy. Of that I am certain. That, and one more thing. Muhammad would never forget the water of life.

3.

Halimah,
the Wet Nurse

I knew it was him kneeling beside my bed. I felt the breeze as he brought the fan close to my face. The palm frond made a soft swishing sound. My eyes were swollen shut by the fever, which is why I didn't see him come in.

"Who's the only woman in your life, Muhammad?" I asked.

"You are."

I smiled through cracked lips. "You're becoming a man if you can lie like that."

We could talk this way, you see, after so many years. The next thing I felt was a cold dampness. He had brought a bowl of water with him and was pressing a cloth to my eyelids, trying to unseal them. They were gummy and swollen. Only the fan managed to keep the flies away.

"Do you remember how small my breasts were?"
I mused.

"Ssh. Drink this."

Muhammad squeezed the cloth so that drops of
water fell on my lips. "What kind of water do you call
this?" I grumbled.

"Holy water, from Zamzam."

I would have spat it back into the bowl if I wasn't
dying of fever. There is no holy water in Mecca, I told
him, only expensive water. He didn't have the money
to waste.

They brought in a doctor with smudge pots last
week to beat back the fever. He burned some dung
chips and threw fresh herbs on them to create a thick,
sweet smoke. That cost money too. You don't get decent
behavior unless you pay, except in the desert.

"Give me my purse," I said. I wanted to pay Muhammad back for the water he squandered his coins
on. In his grandfather's day the tribes paid their family
for water. Not any more. There had been fierce arguing
after "the Slave" died. Now gangs of scowling Qurayshi youths circle the well, holding it hostage until the
disputes are settled. Will they ever be?

"Don't worry," said Muhammad, refusing any
money. Seeing that I could drink a little, he held the
bowl up to my mouth and tipped it. "Between you and

me, I saw a pilgrim who had left a half-full jug on a window sill. I stole some of his water."

I tried to laugh in disbelief, but my throat tightened up, and the laugh turned into a croak. "If you stole, then I marched into the Kaaba and ran away with a big black ram." I painted a picture for Muhammad of what the ram and I did when we got home.

"Don't talk like that," he said.

I don't know why I liked to make him blush. Maybe it made me feel more like his mother, poor soul. I reached up to see if his cheek was hot with embarrassment. I felt something else. A beard was coming on. I turned my head away.

"What's wrong?" he asked.

The young never understand the sadness of growing up. They're too busy doing it. At least my eyes were too swollen to show tears. I said, "Do they still let you tease the girls?" That would be forbidden once he had a real beard.

"I don't tease."

"Oh, then you're holier than your precious water."

There was a loud knock on the door, but nobody came in. Only one visitor a day was allowed. Doctor's orders, to keep the contagion from spreading. Muhammad opened the door a crack, and I heard two male voices. They were impatient. One tried swear-

ing a little. He was just a boy, like Muhammad, but he
needed to practice cursing the same way he needed to
examine his fuzzy beard every morning to see how it
was getting on.

Muhammad had many cousins. At least he enjoyed a
scrap of good fortune. I didn't know all their names. His
father, the cursed Abdullah, had nine brothers, so there
was an army of cousins for him to run with on the streets.
That would go on after teasing the girls had ended.
Growing up never stops a man from prowling the alleys.

I lifted my hand to my breasts. Of course Muhammad didn't remember how small they were that year.
He was barely out of the womb. But it was thanks to
small breasts that he came to me.

Fifteen years ago we made our way to town, as the
desert tribes do every spring. The men had lambs to
sell and the yarn spun by the women over the winter.
They gathered around the Kaaba, and the elders, who
were trusted with the money, gathered at the inns. They
bartered all day, arguing in loud voices. Every once
in a while somebody told a joke, and then the tension
was relieved by laughter. You hear those filthy jokes
all over the world, and the same laughter. Indecency is
how men know that they are men.

Women didn't go into the inns, but we had our own
business. We sat at the gates of the rich families, holding

out our babies and waiting. It was for the milk, you see. City women have babies, but they don't give them the breast. It's not because they're lazy and pampered and don't want sore nipples. They're worried. Living in a city like Mecca, where breathing the air is the same as breathing in contagion, they had to be careful. So every spring we came in from the desert to offer our breasts. That was the custom and still is, although it's on the decline. It's a wonder the air in the city doesn't kill all the babies before they take their first step.

The newborns were put in baskets tied to the sides of the camels, and we took them back to the desert to nurse. In two years time we returned with them, and then the city women, overjoyed to have their children fat and healthy, showered us with coins and gifts. If you ever see a Bedouin woman with silk around her head, you know she's nursed a baby, maybe twins if she is wearing gold earrings.

I had my own boy baby to show them that spring, but times were bad. There had been no rain for months. Everyone's breasts dried up. Mine were half the size they should have been, shrunk like dried dates. I wrapped my robe around myself and held my arms crossed so no one would notice. Who was I fooling? My own baby was shriveled and crying, desperate for the little milk I had. The spoiled rich women walked straight past me without a glance. I spent three days wandering from courtyard to courtyard, without luck. My husband told me to keep trying, but what was the use? We needed the money, of course.

"Muhammad?" I couldn't hear voices at the door and thought he might have slipped out.

"Just here. Don't worry."

He was by my side again. He pushed up my sleeves and began to wash my arms. We kept quiet. For a boy to do that, washing a woman's arms . . . Some people would have frowned, even if I was his milk-mother.

"Open the shutters. It's too hot. It's like a tomb," I said.

"You know I can't do that. It would ruin everything."

The doctor with the smudge pots said that the room had to be kept closed and hot, to drive the fever out. I knew no better. In my delirium, I couldn't even remember being taken to this room. It was small and close; it smelled foul. But Muhammad had no money. With both his parents gone, and now his uncle Abu Talib, he had no right to any fortune. He took what room they gave him for my sickroom.

I wanted to grumble some more, just to hear his voice, but suddenly I was too exhausted. I let my head loll on the pillow while Muhammad finished my arms.

His mother, Aminah, was the only one who didn't shun me the year of my small breasts. The whole town knew about her. Her husband died in caravan, barely two days away from home. Strangers put him in the ground immediately. She never got to throw herself onto his body. I don't think she would have. Her female cousins gathered at her gate to wail with her, but Aminah was a silent widow. No one had seen such a thing. A two-month bride robbed of the best husband in the city? She had to be in shock, they said.

But Aminah could still think. She knew she was being stalked like soft prey. Fate had fixed its eyes upon her. None of the other Bedouin women would come to her house. She didn't have a brass coin to pay for their breasts.

A shadow appeared over me, and it was Aminah. "I have a new baby. Will you come in?" she said in a soft voice. I was squatting at her gate and was almost asleep from fatigue and thirst.

We drank tea without a word. Why speak? We knew we needed each other. I wouldn't beg, and neither would she.

After a while she said politely, "You're slender."

"In our tribe, Banu Sa'd, we work too hard to get fat. Our men are used to it by now," I replied.

I knew what she meant. I loosened my robe and casually bent over the teapot, pretending to wonder if it had steeped too long. She could see for her-self that my breasts didn't hang as fat as they should have.

"May I have two years?" Aminah asked. She had such a small voice, even in her own home. Perhaps she was naturally timid. Or the eyes of fate had broken her.

Two years was the normal time for nursing a baby in the desert. As a precaution I asked to see the baby. She brought it out in swaddling clothes. She said the cloth was soiled and pulled it away. I saw that the baby, tiny and red as a skinned rabbit, had male parts. You understand?

There is another kind of "mother" who comes to the gates of the rich. It doesn't matter what her milk is like, because they hand her an infant wrapped in black cloth, its face covered from sight. Women are weak, even in the desert. If you carry a baby away to leave on the mountainside—always a girl baby—seeing its face might soften your heart. But what good would it do to save them? The boys grow up to a hard life, and many will die before they travel on their first cara-van. Some will never return. A surplus of virgins and widows is the last thing anyone needs. My husband asked if I would serve as such a "mother." I told him I'd rather kill myself. We have a daughter ourselves, don't we?

The contract took only an hour to seal. First I rushed back to camp outside the town walls and got permission from my husband to take the widow's baby. A very grudging permission.

"After two years you'll be lucky to get a silver ring out of it," he said.

"I'm doing this even if I get her cast-off sandals," I replied.

We argued. I insisted. He frowned, but what can you do? We'd get nothing if I left without a baby.

After Aminah had cried a little, the Banu Sa'd passed the city walls at twilight, heading for the open desert. I don't know how sailors feel when they smell the sea again, but it must be like how I feel when I can smell the desert. A funny expression, for in truth you can't smell anything. When the last whiff of rancid smoke, sewage, and dung is out of your nostrils, you are in the desert, where the life is as pure as the air. For the next two years Muhammad never smelled corruption, or saw a house wall for that matter.

My breasts swelled when I began to nurse the new baby. The other women became jealous. They spread rumors that I was feeding him camel's milk. I cornered the worst shrew and showed her my breast.

"See? It got big on its own," I told her and made clear what I would do if she kept up her accusations. The next thing you know, they'll say I made a pact with demons. How could I tell them that it was the baby who brought me so much milk? The udders of the goats and camels also swelled, but no one would believe me if I told them. Milk in the middle of a drought. Who can say why?

"I must go," Muhammad said.

His voice brought me back from my fever dreams. I didn't know how long I had slept. The blackness in that horrible little room was the same, day or night.

Muhammad put his hand on my brow. "Lie still. I won't be long. What can I bring you?"

"Bring me the stars," I mumbled.

Which sounds like I was delirious, but he smiled. Any Bedouin would.

One morning soon after, Muhammad found me sitting up in bed, and when he felt my brow, it was cool and dry. The first thing I wanted wasn't food, even though I was starving. I wanted to be carried outside. Muhammad fetched two of his cousins, and they carried my bed into a dirty courtyard shaded by palm trees. I was puzzled. Why hadn't my people come to carry me?

"The contagion is worse. They had to leave," said Muhammad soberly.

I asked how bad it was. He said people were dying too fast to be buried. The tribes were stacking up corpses outside the city walls. So it was right for my people to flee. They had no reason to lose their lives waiting to see if mine might be saved. Muhammad had girl cousins too, and they brought me millet gruel with lamb in it for strength. They were pretty girls, and gossips. Their chatter was meant to cheer me up, but I sent them away. I didn't need cheering. Hearing the wind in the palms was better than a chorus of blessed spirits.

We Bedouin are proud, but not so proud that we are immune to money. Sometimes foreign traders will ride into camp on half-dead horses. They empty their purses for a goatskin of water and a guide to the next oasis. Most foreigners foolish enough to cross the desert without a Bedouin don't make it to an encampment. We find their remains bleaching on the dunes.

The first time Muhammad saw such a sight he was no more than five. It shocked him. A man's body splayed out on the sand, his skin already turning to parchment, and his horse a hundred feet away, as dead as he was. The wind was mild that day. It had filled their mouths with sand, but not yet covered their bodies.

"There's a fool," I said. "Letting his horse loose. Who would do that?"

"He wanted to be nice," said Muhammad innocently.

I knelt down and looked him in the eye. "No horse can survive on its own out here. What he should have done is kill the horse and climb inside its belly. That way he would have been protected for a day or two." I knew what I was talking about. The Banu Sa'd were close by. We would have seen the vultures circling over the dead animal and come to see. Even after three days a man might be found alive inside a horse or camel. He wouldn't be a pretty sight, but death is much uglier.

Muhammad listened, but his eyes kept wandering to the dead man, whose mouth had gasped open in his last moments, leaving a hole for the sand to fill. You could see the boy wanted to ask me something, but he didn't. I understood. Fate was a tease. Young as he was, he had experienced how cruel a tease. So had his mother. At the end of two years I brought her baby back. Aminah was waiting by the gate and let loose a cry of joy when she saw us coming. Muhammad was walking on sturdy little legs by my side. Bedouin babies don't start to walk when they want to. They start as soon as they have to, which is very early among nomads.

Hearing her cry, Muhammad drew back. He had been taught that this was a sign of danger. The camp is under attack when women sound the alarm. And he didn't know her, of course. To him, I was his mother. I bent down and slapped him hard across the face.

"Go to her. Forget me," I said. "I hate you like a stranger." We always use the same harsh words when giving a baby back. Muhammad didn't move or even cry. He had to be hit a second time before he ran toward Aminah, who was crouching in the street now, arms open wide. But their reunion was a tease. Mecca had been infected with a plague, and when the first neighbor died on Aminah's street, she covered her face with a veil into which bitter herbs were knotted. She veiled her baby's face too, but this was a futile precaution. She knew fate wasn't done with her. In tears she returned Muhammad to me. Contagion blows from house to house faster than dust, so there was little time to consider.

"When should I bring him back?" I asked. I was rushing back to the same camp where the Banu Sa'd always stay, only now it was dangerously close to town. Aminah ran beside me, holding Muhammad in her arms. He couldn't run fast enough to keep up, and she couldn't bear parting from him so soon, after only a day.

I asked again. "Two months, three?" It was up to her.

"Three years. Keep him as long as you can," Aminah said.

I won't lie. I was shocked. "But the plague will be gone once the weak are all dead. It won't take nearly that long, perhaps by winter."

She wasn't listening. She thrust her baby into my arms and ran away, not looking back. Which wasn't heartless, as you might think. She knew what fate was like. It was like a wasp covered in honey. You cannot taste the sweetness without a sting.

That was why the boy grew up to be five among the nomads and saw his first corpse in the sand dunes. Foreigners had other uses besides dying on us, which could be very useful if their horses were still alive and their purses full of coins. Muhammad learned about respect from the eyes of strangers. Not just the ones from outside Arabia, who were forced to show respect unless they wanted to wake up one morning in the desert to find that their guide had disappeared in the night. City Arabs move freely back and forth between the city and the wild. The young men in particular are never more than half tamed by life in town. Since childhood they have heard about falcon hunting and sneak attacks on the tents of the enemy. Young men want glory, and they sneak away into the desert as soon as they can.

Muhammad met many of them from his tribe, the Quraysh, who were the proudest of all, since they were used to power and money in Mecca. It took only a few days to strip their pride. It wasn't done through humiliation or mischief (although no one strongly objected to handing them a blanket full of sand fleas to wrap themselves in at night—a few hundred pink bites is a healthy reminder of how things are). What won their respect was something you'd never suspect: words. The young men come with mouths as filthy as the bottoms of their feet. A few can read, but all know the magic of words, and there is no purer magic than the words of the Bedouin.

We are the living chronicle of every Arab hero and god. Our minds are soaked in poetry the way a wineskin is soaked with juice. Their first night sitting around the fire, the young men are shivering with cold—they never come dressed for the chill that descends after the sun sinks—and exchanging filthy anecdotes to keep warm. No one rebukes them. A Banu Sa'd elder will softly begin to sing one of the songs about a great raid in which our ancestors stole a hundred camels. A second man will join in once he recognizes the tune, then a third. In a few moments the whole tribe is singing, and the young men's jaws drop. It's not the melody or the exploit being praised that moves them, but the strength of every voice singing as one, and in such beautiful, pure Arabic as these corrupt young dandies have never heard in their whole lives.

You think you know what comes next. I will praise Muhammad for being the best singer or the youngest or the most precocious. I will paint a picture of the day he stood up and astonished the men by singing a song he had only heard once, not getting a syllable wrong. In fact, Muhammad almost never sang, except in a low voice no one could hear. When we were blessed by a wandering bard and laid a feast before him in order to hear his epics of massacred Christians and enemy armies drowned in sand overnight, Muhammad sat on the edge of the assembly or even sneaked away. I had to protect him from suspicion that he had blood that wasn't Arab in his veins. Without verse and song, what is an Arab?

No use worrying about that. I was anxious that fate would never let him see his mother again. But after three years they were reunited again. She was waiting by the gate, just as before. She crouched in the street with her arms spread wide. Only this time she didn't cry out, and I didn't slap Muhammad to make him run to her. He was old enough to be told what his situation was. When he set eyes on Aminah, he was prepared for this strange woman who must be called mother. He didn't kiss me, but only gave a grave little bow and walked slowly into her arms.

Aminah brought me inside. She was poorer than ever, but she had cakes and tea waiting for me, and two girls in bangles who did a dance in my honor (they had been coached to run off as soon as they were done, not staying for a share of cake and tea). She placed a small sandalwood box on the table between us. When I opened it, I saw all the jewelry she possessed in the world. One was a single pearl as large as my thumb, which I knew she had brought with her in her dowry when she arrived in the house of Abdullah.

Aminah saw that I was about to protest. She drew Muhammad close and wrapped her skirt around him. "You take it. Now I have a richer pearl," she said. She was a woman, but she had the Arab way with words.

I spent the night in a featherbed covered with a silk spread, once beautiful, now worn almost threadbare. I couldn't sleep, because my mind kept thrashing a memory over. Aminah was eager to know everything about her son, and we had spent the evening in one-sided talk, as I recounted everything he had learned among the Banu Sa'd. But fear forced me to lie. I withheld the one thing she had to be told.

The thing happened when he was three. One day I was scrubbing out a copper pot with sand when my own child, a boy little older than Muhammad, ran into the tent.

"Two men are killing my brother!" he cried.

He was too breathless and frightened to say more. I raised a cry and ran out into the desert, following the tracks my boy had left. A few men heard my distress and joined me. That morning Muhammad had wandered off. We covered a long distance before I spotted him lying in the sand near a thornbush. My heart pounded. I rushed to his side. He was alive, but very weak.

"Run after them! They tried to kill him!" I cried, but the men didn't move. They were bewildered. There was no blood on the boy's body and no wounds. Looking around, you couldn't see tracks leading anywhere. Nobody called my son a liar. We have a good position, and they wouldn't dare. I swept Muhammad up in my arms, grateful that he hadn't gotten lost. Somehow the string that tied him to one of the girls must have broken.

I scolded my boy, and his father threatened to beat him for lying, but he never changed his story. He had followed Muhammad out into the desert when he saw the broken string. The footprints were easy to track. When he came over a rise, he saw two strangers bent over Muhammad, who was lying on his back just as we found him. The two had long knives, and while one kept the boy pinned with his knee, the other plunged his blade into Muhammad's chest. If they noticed that they were being observed, they didn't turn their heads. The one reached into Muhammad's chest and did something. My boy couldn't tell what; he was barely six himself. The sight so frightened him that he watched for only a minute before running back to camp.

The tale was not incredible to everyone. *Jinns* roam the desert thirsting for human souls. That was the strongest possibility. I had my doubts, though. *Jinns* attack at night, and they don't need knives to pluck out your soul. They have dark enchantment. Not that anyone has survived to say what that enchantment is. I feared Muhammad would be shunned for drawing two demons so close to camp in broad daylight. In fact, the opposite happened. The fact that he had survived their attack was considered to be a sign of stronger magic than that of the *jinns*. It was decided that Muhammad's name would be added to the songs about our ancestors who had driven off *jinns*. After that, his reputation was made. Besides, it was obvious he hadn't had his soul sucked out.

I couldn't tell Aminah this, and since Muhammad was so young, there was no fear that he would let it slip. I took the sandalwood box and departed the next morning after first tucking the pearl under Aminah's pillow. Everything in the box would have vanished anyway, once she fell sick and doctors had to be paid.

In the few years she had left, I would have been welcome in her house, but I never went back. Muhammad
had spent enough time with a mother who wasn't real.
Now he needed time with a mother who would be real
such a short time. Aminah was like a shadow passing
through his life.

When he was sure that I had regained my strength,
Muhammad led me from my sickroom to the edge of
town. Mecca is too green to see the desert from, even
atop the highest watchtower. He fussed over my bags
when the small train of donkeys and camels arrived to
take me home. I let him. Why not? A hundred cousins
aren't the same as a milk-mother. My few things were
packed into saddlebags. The Banu Sa'd men who came
for me were old ones who could be spared, and they
hated the city. The circling hills shut out too much of
the sky. In haste I was laid on a stretcher behind the
last camel, since I was too weak to make the journey
on foot. The last thing I felt wasn't love for Muhammad, but a twinge of curiosity.

"Do you remember one day in the desert, when you
were very young and got lost?" I asked.

He nodded. "But I wasn't lost. I had a feeling where
I should go. Two men were waiting for me when I got
there."

I was amazed. "They attacked you, and you never told me? After we got you home, you wouldn't say a word."

"I couldn't. I knew you thought the *jinns* had captured me."

"It had to be *jinns*. They left no footprints. They were seen ripping open your chest."

"I wondered why everyone whispered behind my back. But it wasn't *jinns*. Other beings live in the desert. You should know that."

If it had been anyone else putting me in my place, my nails would have been at his face. But with him I felt a mixture of meekness and wonder. "What kind of beings?" I asked in a small voice.

A strange smile crossed Muhammad's face. "I've never stopped asking that question. You came running in such a panic, you scared them off." He put a finger lightly on his heart. "Don't worry. Whatever they wanted to do, it's done."

4.

Waraqah,
the Believer

The best hiding place is inside your own heart. I've tried all the others. Even when I dug a hole by the open latrines and covered it with thatch, they dragged me out and beat me. I was young then, and they were thugs. A hideous idol with a serpent's tail had been found smashed to bits outside the Kaaba. It was probably one of them, getting drunk and daring one another. But I was easier to blame.

I only wanted to be alone so I could think about God. How did that hurt anyone? But loneliness is the seeker's affliction. It drove me to wander in the marketplace. I was overheard muttering to myself. *Allah, endow my heart with wings, so that I may fly to the garden of eternity.* I meant it as a prayer, but they took it as sacrilege.

One time a scrap of writing fell out of my pocket. Some Qurayshi roughs picked it up, and a wandering scribe recited it aloud: "The veil between God and his servant does not exist in heaven or on earth. It exists in himself." I couldn't dig a hole deep enough to hide that kind of blasphemy.

Eventually I saved my skin by getting rich. Money is protection against persecution. Not perfect protection. If looks could kill, the Qurayshi youth who prowl the streets would send me to a shallow grave every day of the week and twice on feast days.

I straighten my spine and walk past them eyes ahead. Once I reach the inns by the Kaaba, my identity changes. I'm no longer "the believer" who cannot enter a house for dinner without the rooms being disinfected with musk after he leaves. I turn into a well-padded merchant whose shameful ideas are insignificant, once you hear the clink of gold in his purse.

"Waraqah ibn Nawfal, you are most welcome."

"Waraqah, my brother, sit here next to me."

"Waraqah, blessed by the gods, make me happy by sharing this wine."

I never trusted any of them, and yet one time I let my guard down. My only excuse is gathering age. I took one of the Quraysh aside, a young man who stood out for being slightly more thoughtful than his peers. I unfolded a parchment before his eyes. It was wrinkled and yellow; it had been clumsily mended in several places.

"What do you think of this?" I asked.

The young man was barely literate, but he looked impressed. "Your will?" he guessed. He was an old camel trader's son, not yet twenty. He probably dreamed about his inheritance every spare moment.

I smiled. "It's more precious than my will. It's a page from the Bible. I've been translating it."

His eyes widened. "Better be careful," he warned. I had pushed the page toward him, but he backed away as if I were offering him a hot coal.

It was comical, really. Everyone knows that such pages exist. A merchant whose route passes through the tiny communities of Jews and Christians may buy or sell an occasional tattered leaf from their jumbled scriptures. But we Arabs pretend that these communities have not sprung up in our midst. It would be like admitting a growth of black smut in your bags of wheat.

I reverently kissed the parchment. "It tells of Abraham and Isaac. You should let me recite the story to you sometime. There's almost a murder in it. You like knives, don't you?" I was toying with the young man, who looked relieved when I folded the scrap and thrust it back into my robe. I was lucky. He could have led a move against me.

What does "the believer" believe? No one ever asks me to my face. They only know that the idols are good business, and anyone who speaks out against them threatens everybody's income. "Listen to reason, my dear Waraqah," they say. "We will shrivel like a barren womb. Mecca will die without the pilgrims. You see how much they spend."

It's true. You can get money out of a pilgrim simply for letting him set eyes on a golden idol. They spend even more during the Hajj, when hundreds flood Mecca to run the circle around the Kaaba. No one knows when that started, but now it's a fixed tradition.

I am approaching Muhammad, my spiritual son, in this roundabout way, because that is how he approached me.

One day, it was a dozen years ago, I was sitting in my courtyard. I was expecting a messenger momentarily and left the gate open. A little boy wandered inside. We looked at each other. I asked where his mother was, but he didn't reply. He gazed at me shyly. From his dress I saw that he must be a nomad. They are fierce about keeping their children close by.

I went over and crouched in front of him. "Do you know me?" I asked. I had the strangest feeling.

He shook his head. "I don't know you, but I hear your voice."

Well, of course he did. I had just spoken to him. But the boy didn't mean that. He turned and pointed past the gate. "I was playing by the well, and I heard you. What do you want?"

If he meant Zamzam, it was ten streets away. "I don't want anything from you," I said, feeling very queer talking this way to a five- or six-year-old.

"Then I must want from you," he said.

Before I could question him, one of those Qurayshi toughs was at my gate. He didn't dare come through it, but he started yelling. "Hey, hey, he's here. I found him."

A second later two of his fellows ran up and behind them a Banu Sa'd woman, red-faced and puffing. "Muhammad!" she cried and rushed into the courtyard to sweep him up. Immediately she realized her discourtesy and began spewing apologies, tangled with a disjointed tale about bringing the boy back to his mother, who hadn't seen him in three years. I didn't care. I assured her that her infraction was nothing. I escorted her back to the gate, glaring at the Qurayshi roughnecks, who lingered in case I gave them a coin. If I didn't, they'd shake down the poor woman, so I slipped them the smallest piece of silver I had. Why not? God sees every good deed.

A tiny incident, but it preyed on my mind. Muhammad had wandered away from his wet nurse when her back was turned and headed straight for my gate.

Under my bed I have many pages of the Bible stashed away. It's my habit to pull one out late at night and translate a few passages into Arabic. I also have another ritual that I keep to myself, for good reason. When I am puzzled over a mystery, large or small, I pull a sheet out at random, and whatever my eye falls upon I take to be a message. A few days after the boy appeared, I reached under the mattress and took out the first page my fingers touched. I shut my eyes and pointed to a passage at random, then took it over to the lamp to read:

Behold, a virgin shall conceive and bear a son,
And his name shall be called Emmanuel.

These were not meaningless words. The man who sold me this particular page was a Christian beggar who followed my caravan many years ago. I threw him some bread, and as he wolfed it down he told me about his savior. He felt blessed, even though he lived in the gutter and fought with stray dogs over garbage.

The year the beggar sold me this scrap of scripture he had a terrible cough. He knew he wasn't long for this world. This page from the Bible was precious to him, and the beggar wanted the message of his Messiah carried forward.

So I knew that the virgin had conceived, and Emmanuel had come. It happened long ago, and the only reason to keep the page was to remind me of how the beggar's face glowed when he spoke about his savior. Why, then, had my finger landed on this verse?

Several years passed before a Jew came to Mecca whom I could trust. He plied gold and silver trinkets. His trade was so valuable that he bought his way out of the law that kept Jews from entering Mecca. I gave him wine and showed him the passage. The name Emmanuel brought a crooked smile to his face.

"Don't trust your beggar," he said. "What kind of a savior would allow someone to live like that?"

The messiah is yet to come, he said, to kill the enemies of the Jews and save them all. I was too impatient to wait that long, I told him. In Arabia, idols can save you today, if you're gullible enough. I pressed the Jew for an explanation that meant something real. More than a bit exasperated, he said that for my understanding "Emmanuel" meant the "king of prophets."

Ah, well, that was a different story.

Arabs put great store in prophets. If God pointed to the word "prophet" when I asked about Muhammad, something must be afoot. In Mecca some of the ignorant call me "the Jew," but that's just their crude way of insulting a servant of God. I have no religion. I am *hanif,* a believer without a faith, like a lone palm tree without an oasis.

I did not approach Muhammad the whole time he was growing up. That was far too risky. I watched from afar. Old Muttalib, his grandfather, was still alive then. It was a tragedy that he had survived his youngest son, Abdullah, but he found solace in Muhammad. He would take the boy to the inns and prop him on his knee while holding forth. Muttalib had gotten too old for trading. He was half blind and growing weaker by the month. It was a common sight, he and the boy, who kept his eyes on the ground. No one had ever seen a child who wanted to keep to himself so much. But Muhammad was obedient, and when Muttalib wanted to show him off, he would stand up like a man, even in front of half a dozen drunk Quraysh in a dingy, smoky wine house.

Then a peculiar thing happened. Many years later I was out walking and happened to see a figure crouched in an alley. The light was dim, but I made out Muhammad squatting on his heels. I nodded. He put his fingers to his lips and pointed at something on the ground. A mouse. The creature had been lured out into the open with a few grains of wheat.

Then Muhammad gazed up at the sky, where a black speck hovered. My eyes were failing, but I knew it was a hawk. Muhammad looked back at the mouse, then at the hawk again.

"It has no idea of the danger," he said.

"Neither do we," I replied.

You see the point? Like the mouse innocently eating its seeds, we go about our lives not realizing that death is watching us from afar, constantly stalking. Those were Muhammad's inner thoughts. Why had he shared them with me? Our voices made the mouse scurry back into its hole. Muhammad stood up and walked toward me.

"I'm a man now," he said. "We can talk."

"A man? You're seventeen," I smiled.

He didn't smile back. "Old enough to defend myself, if anyone catches us talking like this."

That's how it started. I never brought up the day his nurse lost him and he wandered into my courtyard, but he must have remembered. What kind of patience does it take to wait twelve years before speaking to someone again? He began coming to my house for tea and God. Only tea at first, because God remained a forbidden subject until later.

Naturally, he wanted to know about me. "What is a *hanif*?" he asked.

"One who believes in Allah, one who scorns idols and waits for the light to descend," I said.

He nodded gravely. "Everyone says you're different, but you look ordinary to me."

Muhammad said this frankly and without apology, considering he was insulting an elder. I answered with a quote from one of my hidden books. "A man goes in and out among the people. He eats and sleeps with them. He buys and sells in the marketplace. This everyone can see. What they cannot see is that he never forgets God for a single instant."

"Are you that man?" asked Muhammad.

"I will be, when I become a saint. For now, I can only try."

"Why is one god better than many?" he asked.

I answered with another question. "Why is one faithful wife better than many whores?"

"What makes you call the gods whores?"

"In both cases you pay your money and get your wish. Only a whore is more reliable and trustworthy. Most idols take your money and give nothing in return," I replied.

Muhammad seemed pleased that I spoke so freely. As for myself, I often had to conceal a burning excitement that agitated me every time I set eyes on him. How could I explain it? It was impossible. I would lose all respect. A grown man trembling like a bride waiting in the dark for her bridegroom.

We talked about everything, endlessly. Yet I could never draw Muhammad out about his own beliefs. This was a cause for concern. In Arabia, one belief swallows up every other: the tribe. The tribe tells you where you belong on earth. The tribe runs to defend you after you knife a stranger for spitting on your sandals. Like a monster with a thousand heads, the tribe sees everything and can eat whom it pleases. There is no room for belief in anything else, including God. God is just another thing for the monster to devour.

One day I'd had enough. I turned on Muhammad. "Talking to you is like talking to a respectful oyster. Open up. Who are you?"

He didn't look startled. "I am one who selects friends carefully."

An angel must have seen my impatience, because at that moment he brought me the perfect response. It was from an old verse. "I have a friend, and he fills my cup with wine that has no equal."

Muhammad blushed. "You have been such a friend to me."

After that, our bond was sealed. We became bold enough that we'd talk in public, late at night after everyone else had stumbled home. I was always eager for his company.

Word soon shot around town that he was my protégé. Just in case anyone took that amiss, I spread my money around more generously. I even sent a messenger boy to buy a calf and sacrifice it outside the Kaaba during the spring rites. He took my money and an hour later came racing back.

"Which god is it for?" the boy asked. "They want to know."

"The one whose only name is 'the One,'" I said. The boy looked confused, so I said, "The choice is theirs. Just make a good show of it." He ran away still confused. No matter. I was used to being unfathomable.

Muhammad was balm to my soul. I had someone to hold in a spiritual embrace. The affliction of loneliness was lifted. But what good was I doing for him? I could always leave him my money. Mecca would have a second rich outcast. There had to be something else.

"Are there other *hanif*?" he asked me one day.

"You mean others who know better how to keep their mouths shut?"

He smiled. "I was thinking of those who might have a taste for wisdom."

"Wisdom is like hot coals," I said. "People enjoy the glow, but they're not stupid enough to step in."

It was the most cynical thing I'd ever said, and his face fell.

"You make me talk like a whore," I murmured, and Muhammad knew it was an apology. We both knew I wasn't ashamed to be a believer. But I never took him to meet another *hanif*. It was contradictory. Two *hanif* make a congregation, three a tribe, and four a faith to be defended against other faiths with arrows and spears. Each *hanif* travels alone, I told him, and it seemed that Muhammad was satisfied with that explanation.

Something gnawed at me, though. I pondered a long time, until I convinced myself that he needed to know about the verse my finger had lighted upon. *And he shall be called Emmanuel.* If I didn't tell him, I would be hiding a great secret from him. The only way to bring up the subject was indirectly. One blazing afternoon we were lying in the courtyard on straw pallets that had been soaked down with water.

Muhammad raised himself up on his elbows. "What is it?"

I faced him. "What do you know about how your father died?"

For once the cautious youth looked startled. "I know he went on a journey and never returned."

"There's more," I said. "Much more."

Muhammad hesitated. He didn't want his memories disturbed, I could tell.

"They aren't your memories," I said. "You never met him. He's like water that someone else has drunk."

"But he was loved," said Muhammad.

That much was undeniable. From the day he was born, Abdullah had led a charmed life. Everyone said so, and that made it so. He was never insulted in the street by a reckless young tough or called out to a fight. He basked in the illusion that he was the first person ever to be loved.

"He wanted to be a hero," I began. "A man who spoke like thunder and laughed like the sunrise. I knew him and saw what his imagination was like. He loved the Bedouin, and he envisioned himself in one of their legends." I eyed Muhammad sharply. "Do you know why your father failed?"

"Because he died."

"No. Because it was not God's will."

Then and there I unfolded the twisted whole story of Abdullah's death, which had been carefully kept from his son.

Everything revolved around Zamzam. The joy that Abdul Muttalib felt when he rediscovered the well was short-lived. He became entangled in Qurayshi intrigues. He was resented for grabbing the rights to the sacred water, and in time Muttalib felt that his enemies would prevail. What he needed was ten strong sons, or so he convinced himself. But the gods had favored him so far with only one.

He spent his days and nights chewing over his obsession, until the situation took a desperate turn. Muttalib went to the Kaaba and gazed at the hundreds of idols that lined the chamber. All at once he believed in none of them. In despair he called on God instead. Deep inside every Arab is an ancestral memory of Allah. It was Allah, the one God, who had led Hagar and Ishmael, the very founders of the Arab race, to Mecca.

Muttalib had never considered Allah reliable enough. The creator of the world had lost interest in his creation. Why else did ill fortune and calamities befall his children? But Muttalib had to have those ten sons, and it was in God's power to grant them. Muttalib knew nothing of Jewish or Christian beliefs. He knew, however, that every god loved sacrifices in his name.

The greatest of the gods would require the greatest sacrifice, he reasoned. Muttalib raised his arms to heaven and promised the most dreadful sacrifice possible, if only he was granted the blessing of ten strong sons to defend him from his enemies.

A decade passed. One after another Muttalib's wives bore him healthy, well-formed sons, until the number reached ten. He was well satisfied, and his peace of mind was all the more profound, because he had forgotten his oath to Allah long ago.

But God can reach into any man's heart. One day while walking to the Kaaba, where the most revered idol was Hubal, the moon god, Muttalib had a vision in bloody detail of his promised sacrifice. He had sworn an oath to give God back one of his sons if he was granted ten. Muttalib was horrified by the picture of himself cutting the throat of one of his precious sons, but the thought of reneging on his promise to God was more horrifying.

He called his sons together and told them that one must die the very next day. But which one? The room fell silent. The sons were as superstitious as the father. They knew the oath had to be carried out. The next day they all gathered inside the Kaaba beside the statue of Hubal. Muttalib believed that if his sons drew lots, Hubal had enough power to select the right one. As you can see, Muttalib was fickle. One day he shivered before the might of God, but when it came to practical affairs, throwing the choice onto an idol's shoulders was easier. He had been paying off Hubal for years.

The sons each wrote their name on an arrowhead and threw the arrows into a quiver. Muttalib reached in and, begging Hubal for guidance, pulled one out.

The name on it was Abdullah's. The other nine sons, needless to say, were relieved, yet no one expected that Muttalib's favorite son would ever be drawn. When the news was announced outside the Kaaba, the gathered crowd began to shout, demanding Muttalib to foreswear his oath. The wife who had borne Abdullah was named Fatimah. She was popular with the common folk, and most of the crowd came from her clan.

Muttalib heard the vociferous protestations with a heart of stone. He had picked a spot between two large idols where he would shed Abdullah's blood. With his unsheathed knife he made his way through the mob. Abdullah followed, white as a ghost. Hands plucked at garments; cries filled the air.

Pardon me if this tragic moment suddenly turns comic, but at the last minute a voice in the crowd shouted, "The gods love money. Pay them off. You can afford it."

Muttalib whirled around in a rage, trying to spot the one who had cried out so insolently. But a tiny voice in his head whispered, *It's not such a bad idea. You're rich, and you love Abdullah more than anyone else in the world.*

With a great show of reluctance Muttalib agreed to spare Abdullah, but there were two details to settle, for now this had turned into haggling. How much should be paid to ransom his son, and who should decide that the price was fair? Since Fatimah's clan had raised such a ruckus, Muttalib forced them to add their money to his. As for an arbiter, it was decided to seek the advice of Shiya, a woman soothsayer who was the most trusted among the various shamans, fortune tellers, astrologers, oracles, and diviners trusted by the Quraysh.

Shiya was a recluse living in the faraway town of Yathrib. The journey had its perils, and Yathrib was traditionally a rival to Mecca in prestige and power. Even so, Muttalib made the trip with a light heart, overjoyed to circumvent his bargain with Allah. It wasn't a good sign that Shiya had just left town when he arrived, but Muttalib brushed this omen off. He traveled a hundred miles north before he found her, an old crone shuttered inside a hovel. She refused him entrance, but after two days of his wheedling Shiya promised to divine an answer.

Her answer was this: "In your tribe, Abdul Muttalib, if a man kills another man, the victim's life is worth ten camels, which are paid to his family. Payment in camels will satisfy the gods in this case too."

Muttalib had his doubts that Allah could be bribed with ten camels, but before he could object, Shiya stopped him. "Take two arrows and go before Hubal again. On one arrow write 'Abdullah' and on the other, 'camels.' Draw out the arrows as you did before, and every time your son's name comes up, add ten more camels to the price. Do this until the word 'camel' is drawn, and you'll have the price the gods demand."

Muttalib and his companions returned to Mecca, and a great crowd gathered for the drawing, laughing and carousing as if this were a feast day. The first arrow that Muttalib drew had Abdullah's name on it, so the price was ten camels. He drew again. Abdullah's name appeared. The price was now twenty camels. The crowd's cheerful banter turned to silence and finally grim-faced awe. Abdullah's name was drawn ten times in a row. The price was a hundred camels, almost the wealth of a well-to-do trader. Muttalib was richer than that, but he blanched.

At last the word "camel" came up on the eleventh try, but by then Muttalib was dejected and overwhelmed with doubts. He stood up before the crowd and raised his hands.

"Draw again," he cried. "If Abdullah's name comes up three times in a row, I will obey the soothsayer. If not, my duty to God forces me to keep my bargain."

This was terrible news to Fatimah's clan and to Abdullah, of course, who let drop a cup of wine he had raised to his lips.

Despite the hue and cry and the horror on Abdullah's face, Muttalib stood firm. All along he had mistrusted

Shiya, suspecting that she might be toying with him because her allegiance was to the tribes of Yathrib.

The arrows were drawn again. One, two, three. An exultant cry rose up from the crowd, because Abdullah's name had appeared on all three draws. His life was spared, and his father paid a hundred camels to the priests at the Kaaba in the name of Hubal.

When I reached this point in my tale, I glanced at Muhammad, who had grown very still. No one had recounted these details to him, and he was steeling himself, since he already knew that his father's reprieve led to no happy ending.

I went on. To celebrate his escape from death, Abdullah was allowed to marry, and at age twenty-five he took Aminah, the daughter of a prominent family in Mecca. They spent three days ensconced in her father's house after the wedding ceremony. But Muttalib had been harboring dark thoughts amid the celebrations. He called Abdullah to him and told him that he should travel by caravan to Syria. The young bridegroom was baffled. Why should he leave? He had only been married a week. The young couple were enjoying the first sweet taste of their love.

Muttalib gave no reasons. He forced his will upon Abdullah, as was his right as the young man's father. With tears and rending cries Aminah ran to the gate clutching Abdullah's robe as he left for Syria. They had been together as man and wife for only two weeks. Abdullah knew that his father was daring God to harm him. It was the old man's way of testing if he had truly fulfilled his oath to Allah. That, and Muttalib's fear that Abdullah's happiness was too great. Between having his life saved and his bliss with Aminah, Abdullah was tempting the gods to destroy him.

"And they did," said Muhammad interrupting.

Abdullah never made it back home. The trading in Syria went well, but his yearning to be back with his bride was strong. Retracing his steps, he passed through Yathrib. There, where Shiya had saved him from fate, Abdullah fell ill with a malady no healer could treat. He died a few days later and was quickly buried, in case his curse happened to be contagious.

"I don't tell you all this to add to your sorrows," I said. "You had to know these things. Abdullah had a sixth sense. He knew that God's will cannot be bargained with. Just as we accept life from Allah, so must we accept death, as a gift that is not ours to question."

Muhammad hadn't waited for the end of my tale before springing to his feet. He began to pace restlessly. "You want to curse my whole family? You might as well with this tale."

A voice told me to keep quiet. Nothing hurt more than Muhammad's anger. Yet stinging words poured from my lips. "This has nothing to do with me. Your mother took you on a trip when you were six. Where? To that same town, Yathrib. She died on the way home, just like her husband. Open your eyes. See the will of God. Accept it."

Muhammad remained silent, but his eyes told a story of defiance.

I continued. "My son, you are fated. I have prayed over you, and God has prepared you for greatness. A great man learns through calamity. It fixes his gaze on heaven, if he is wise."

The color rose in Muhammad's cheeks. "You made my father and his father out to be mere dreamers."

"Sometimes dreamers see more than ordinary people," I replied. "Abdullah fled his young bride even though it broke her heart. He ushered himself off the scene before it was done for him."

I had gone too far. Another youth might have tightened his fists and started swearing. Muhammad stopped pacing and gazed at me. I put my hand on his shoulder to calm him.

"I'm saying that all men must die, but some may go to their deaths willingly as a sacrifice. In that way they become true servants of God. We never know the truth until it is revealed."

Muhammad pulled away. He was too upset to listen and ran toward the courtyard gate. I didn't call after him. Without using the word "prophet," I had opened the possibility of a special fate. Muhammad didn't return the next day, or the day after that. He avoided contact, only nodding at me if our paths happened to cross at the inns or near the Kaaba. His gaze was strangely guilty. It would be months before he relented and asked to see me again.

The night I revealed Muhammad's destiny to him I couldn't sleep. I pulled out a page from my hidden cache and pointed a finger in the dark. When I brought it close to the lamp, the words beneath my finger brought consolation.

For strait is the gate, and narrow is the way that leads to life, and few there be who find it.

5.

Barakah,
the African Slave

I don't know if hell has three circles, but Mecca does. The first ring is where the rich live, the second is for those who dream of getting rich, and the third is for the dregs, who wait upon the first two. I live in the worst, the farthest circle away from God. All around me, desperation is a way of life. In a drought I've seen children squat to sip from the sewer. The rich would rather kiss a leper than come to the filthy alleys where our crumbling hovels stand. They crowd around the Kaaba, their mansions and courtyards shouldering each other aside like old women grabbing for peaches in the bazaar.

Is my head less blessed, because it's not covered with silk?

"Barakah, I trust you. You're the only one I trust," says Muhammad.

He comes to see me. That's proof that he's not rich yet. Ever since old Muttalib died, their clan has fallen. Slaves found themselves thrown out on the street, begging for a master to feed them. It's shocking how the vultures closed in, stripping the Hashim of power, forcing them into humiliation. Muhammad did what he had to. He began to trade his small fund, and that has served him well. I never thought he'd reach twenty without begging for help.

His visits to me aren't planned. He drops in on hell when the mood strikes him. God seal my mouth for saying such things. He loves me—that's the real reason. I was the first person to hold him when he was born. I belonged to his mother, the lady Aminah, in those days. I've been passed along so many times I couldn't name all my owners. I'm like a water skin that won't be thrown out until it leaks its life away.

One day I look up from sweeping the blown dirt and leaves from my last master's courtyard, and I see an amazing sight. Muhammad leading a caravan, and so young. An older merchant weary of travel trusted him to go in his place. When he spots me from atop his camel, he gives me a serious nod. I know Muhammad wants to dismount and embrace me, but he can't, not in front of men he gives orders to. In the back of my mind I think, *Your father never returned, your mother never returned. Maybe the curse ended with them.*

And he did return. Word spread that Muhammad could be trusted to keep his head in dangerous corners. He will soon have the money to buy me for himself.

"Money?" I laugh. "No master will give me shelter anymore. You can have me for free."

Muhammad winces, but we both know what is lacking. He first needs a wife. A female slave in a single man's house is scandalous. Everyone would know what she's really there for. Gossips would say that he likes them old.

"How did you become so respectable?" I tease Muhammad.

"Don't worry. It's a disguise," he jokes back. Walking past him in the street, you see Muhammad's hair and beard cut like those of someone who's prosperous. He wears a cloak dyed in rich blue and trimmed with braid. Only I know what he is. He allows me to stroke his cheek to feel how perfectly the razor has done its work. And why not? I ushered him into this world, a squealing naked creature. His respectability ends at my doorstep.

"You've come to save me," I murmur. "You've come to save everybody."

"Don't be foolish," he replies. "I'm as helpless as anyone, and even more confused."

I shake my head. "Wine ferments before it grows sweet. That's what you're doing. The sweetness will come."

I think our intimacy pleases him. I wouldn't be in danger if I shouted about it from the rooftops. That's one advantage of being invisible. All poor women are invisible here, except in bed. For half an hour they are divine creatures then. What does that make me, twice as invisible? I was born a slave, and I sleep alone.

The memory of Muhammad's mother haunts me. Aminah worshiped Abdullah beyond the grave. The gods were displeased; Abdullah was her only idol. She took that final trip beyond Yathrib to weep over the pile of stones where they buried him. When she turned her steps back to Mecca, a full month later, grief had destroyed her health. I was walking ahead of her donkey when I heard Aminah say, as softly as a frightened child, "We stop here." She felt sick. Walking beside her, Muhammad hung his head.

I felt a shiver run down my spine. Two women and a six-year-old boy pitching a tent alone in the desert? We got it up somehow, and Aminah crawled inside, as if the tent's folds could protect her from a trembling fever. She died so quickly. I barely had time to send

Muhammad out of the tent, but he couldn't stand it and ran back inside, just in time to fling himself on his mother's unconscious body. We wailed together like wounded animals, then buried her with our own hands. The whole way home the boy kept staring at the dirt under his torn, ragged fingernails. The dirt of his mother's grave. What a horrible thing to set your eyes upon.

I had my own horrors. Watching a young woman die like that, burning up in my arms, was worse than seeing your house burn down. This was a soul turned to ashes. Aminah begged me to take care of her boy. I did what I could. For a while it was possible. Old Muttalib took me into his house. I didn't have to live in hell then. I had a tiny room at the back of his rambling mansion. He loved Muhammad so much that he even pushed out an old crone who had inhabited the room like a forgotten ghost. I shudder to think of where she went. But Muttalib died, and his sons lost the power. I cried to lose Muhammad, who was only eight. He went into Abu Talib's house, a small dwelling where the clink of gold was rarely heard.

I can't remind Muhammad of these things or he blushes with shame. "I should have gone with you on to the street," he says. However, we both know that was impossible.

When he arrives in his fancy blue robes, the braid dragging in the dust because he doesn't pay attention, my boy brings me bread, olives, and a small clay jar of oil. I don't dive into it. The way the vulgar rich tear at their food disgusts me. I taught Muhammad better, and I've seen him sit quiet and hungry while Abu Talib's sons clawed at the dinner bowls like hyenas. With the food Muhammad brings, we sit opposite each other on a tattered rug and nod politely for the other to go first.

"Here," he says once, holding out a small glass vial. You didn't even have to take out the stopper to smell what it was. Attar of rose. I thought I'd faint from intoxication.

"Open it," he urges, when I shove the vial into my underblouse.

"Don't be silly. It will attract flies, and I have enough as it is." But I was just trying to keep from crying in front of him.

As Muhammad has grown, he has become more troubled. One day I ask him about this. "To be empty is to be miserable," he says, which makes no sense

And now the bad times have come. People are afraid. You have to know how to read the signs. One day I'm walking along and what do I see? The sand outside a rich man's gate is bloody. It's not brown blood, the leftovers of a street fight. It's shockingly red and fresh.

Usually everyone looks away when there's blood. To stare might mean you've got an opinion about the fight, and anyone with an opinion has taken sides, a dangerous thing to do in Mecca.

On this day I hear buzzing in the air. People aren't just staring; they're talking angrily, and I see something else. The trail of blood leads into the rich man's courtyard. This wasn't just a common knife fight between two young hotheads.

I know instantly what it means. The balance has been wrecked. The rich are protected from losing their blood, unless the tribes can't settle their differences behind closed doors. Once there is chaos, no one is safe.

"Come away. You can't stay here," a voice says, and I feel someone pulling at my elbow. By now the buzzing voices are thicker, like flies around a dead animal, but I see that it's Muhammad, and I let him drag me off.

"I've seen riots," I say, because, to tell you the truth, I wanted to stay and watch. Not for the sake of more blood. I've seen women bloodied by their husbands more times than I can remember. All this cruelty is a kind of vanity, if you ask me. A man brags in the inns that he's a bull in bed when his wife knows he's a rabbit. So she has to pay. A crazy world, when one gets punished for another's shame. I wanted to stick around to find out who the new victims were going to be. If the clans are jockeying for power, the losers aren't the ones you want to serve.

When he gets me to a side street, Muhammad looks worried. He warns me not to go near that house again. I shrug. It doesn't matter that much where you go when you're invisible, but he repeats the warning and tells me there are three other houses I must not be seen around.

"Everyone watches. They know who goes through those gates," he says.

"I'll go where I please," I say. Which is a boastful way of reminding him that wherever my master sends me, I have to go. I have to obey.

"You won't be sent there anymore," he replies. His voice is grim, but he won't explain what he means. As we part at the corner, Muhammad leaves me with strange words: "The dawn doesn't come back to awaken us twice."

I feel prickly all over when he says that, but before I can question him, he has melted into the crowd. Now, you'd think something dark was afoot. Maybe one night the vigilantes will raid a particular clan and wipe out all the young males. It's happened before, and since they sometimes get careless and slit the throats of a few slaves, I keep to my house the next few nights, begging off that it's my unclean days of the month.

The buzzing won't die down. The next time I carry a basket of washing to the well, I stand next to an Abyssinian woman I know; it's easier next to another black. They leave us alone. And she says, "You won't believe it. Uthman wants to be king. That's why they nicked him with a knife. It happened while he was coming home. He screamed blue murder and ran inside."

"They did more than nick him," I say, slapping the laundry harder against the rim of the well to make more noise. It wouldn't do to be overheard.

"That's not the point. A king—these Arabs won't stand for it."

A few eyes dart our way, so we shut up. But to tell the truth, I feel like laughing. A crazy man calls himself a king. I call myself Queen of the Nile, but the last time I looked, there isn't a crown under my pillow.

Muhammad doesn't smile when I bring it up, however. "Uthman bin al-Huwayrith. He's not crazy. He just doesn't know how to keep a secret."

The Arabs love secrecy more than they love a feud even. They have a saying: "A secret is like a bird. Let it go from your hand, and it flies everywhere."

Gravely Muhammad tells me that Uthman has become a Christian. He looks surprised when I burst out laughing.

"Is that all?" I say. The last thing a slave has to worry about is who to worship. Our masters point to their idols, and there's an end to it. We bow down where they bow down.

"I wish you could understand," Muhammad murmurs.

"Why?"

"Because Uthman has brought the pot to a boil. Not just him. There are others. They refuse to hide anymore."

I settle down for Muhammad's sake and pay attention.

"This Uthman is a rich Qurayshi. He got drunk one night and declared that the lands beyond Arabia are civilized. They have laws. A man's money is as safe there as his life. He can even loan with interest, like the Jews. That made the others sit up, even though they don't tolerate words against their damned pride. Uthman explained that the Christians are the true sons of Abraham, them and the Jews. If Mecca had a Christian king, trade would improve for everyone. Alliances could be made with Byzantium, where Christians pile gold as high as a virgin's head to make her dowry. 'Oh, and who would be king?' someone yelled in derision. Which is where Uthman should have shut his big mouth. 'Make me king,' he shouted over the general laughter. 'I'm a Christian already.'

"Uh-oh. The room grew quiet. Everyone knew there were *hanif* around, and it was assumed that Uthman was one. He went freely to and from the house of Waraqah. But Uthman tried to wave a big stick and accidentally hit a hornet's nest. He upset the balance, and over such a stupid thing. They warned him with a nick, but then some others came out on his side, and they were mumbling about Christians and Jews too, saying that they're all the true sons of Abraham."

"Why not go and ask Abraham himself?" I say, growing bored with the tale.

Muhammad gives a small, crooked smile. "If only we could." He explains that Abraham is the grandfather of grandfathers, and no one knows how long ago he lived or who his true sons are, except that part of keeping power for the Quraysh meant that they laid claim to him. He says that if they aren't the sons of Abraham, they're just another tribe of puffed-up bullies.

"Are you taking sides?" I ask Muhammad. And he drops a saying: "A lizard doesn't hop from one branch until he's sure of the next one." Arabs live by old sayings. I shouldn't criticize. Muhammad is being prudent. He's known for that. He's earned more money by refusing the third cup of wine than by shrewdness.

"This won't go away," says Muhammad, getting up and leaving me the last piece of bread. "Zamzam ran underground out of sight for a long time. No one knew it was there until my grandfather had a vision. God has been running underground too. He hasn't broken through yet, but the ground is moist, and everyone can see it."

"You can't drink moist dirt," I point out. Muhammad smiles and leaves.

6.

Khattab,
the Elder

Years ago Christ's army marched on Mecca to destroy us, and almost succeeded. Memories are short. People talk about the trouble being stirred up now. This is nothing compared to the madness back then. I pulled Muhammad into my house to make him listen. His influence is growing in the tribe. He understands trade, and I trade in power. If Mecca collapses, the Arabs will be powerless. We are devouring ourselves.

"Once you hear me out, you can alert the others," I began. "You are young, but your counsel means something."

"Am I here for a history lesson?" Muhammad asked with a serious smile.

"It's a lesson about danger," I said. "Last time the danger came from without. This time it festers within, like a disease. I feel the plague spreading. Trust me, I've seen the worst."

Muhammad bowed and took a seat. "Tell me."

I cast my mind back. "News spread of an attacker marching across the desert. Bedouin boys tending sheep in the mountains were the first to spot the enemy. They ran to town crying that huge monsters were in league with thousands of soldiers. Mecca had no defenses. Our men couldn't form a proper army. The desert has protected us for so long, they had forgotten what war was like. This devil Christ must have been protecting his soldiers to bring them across a hundred miles of sand without dying of thirst. Panic broke out. Everyone became a nomad overnight. The clans ran into the desert to escape the invaders. People said hysterical things: Christ's followers ate human flesh; the Jews had sold them secret plans to the city. Doors were marked with signs in blood in the dead of night."

"It must have been horrible," said Muhammad. He was listening, but you never knew what he was thinking, not that one.

"Horrible? You've never stared starvation in the face, you and your generation. The bazaar was stripped clean as if by a swarm of locusts. A few sellers tried gouging. They offered a pomegranate in trade for a pearl. Instead, men held knives to their throats and stole the pomegranate. They deserved it too."

Muhammad nodded. He never faltered in the respect department. However, the real question remained. Would Muhammad stand with us, the guardians?

I take some wine at noon for my blood, and it can go to my head. I found myself shouting at him. "This must never happen again, do you understand? Never!"

"Is that why you had Uthman attacked?" he asked in a voice as quiet as mine was loud. "Is he part of the disease?"

"Nobody had anybody attacked," I muttered resentfully.

"Did the knife go in on its own?"

"Uthman is a secret Christian," I said. "You don't understand. And since you have eyes in your head, that means you refuse to understand. Let everything crash. I'm old. What does it matter?"

I slumped back on a pile of cushions and poured myself another cup. There was nothing more to say. Muhammad gazed out the window. I stared into the dregs of the wine and swatted a fly. It was too hot to argue. If Mecca goes to hell, they can't blame me.

"I admire you," said Muhammad suddenly.

I was so startled, all I could blurt out was, "Why?"

"'Fate loves a rebel.' You know that saying?" he asked.

"I'm not the rebel. Things are going on behind closed doors. Conspirators are trying to destroy us. Fanatics, zealots. If they have their way, another army of demons will be at our walls."

Muhammad didn't cringe. I wasn't so drunk that I didn't know I was losing my case. I couldn't live with myself if the blame fell on me. To calm my nerves, I retold the story of Christ's invasion. I assumed Muhammad had already heard it, but I needed to tell it and he needed hear it again.

"You were born that year. I knew your mother, as I knew all of the clan of your great-grandfather Hashim. Her belly was swollen when I came to warn her. Aminah wasn't the kind to be hysterical. She wanted to know everything, so I talked to her as if she was a man."

My words were pouring out freely, but I was far away. In my mind's eye I could see her again, clutching her robe around her throat so that her hand wouldn't tremble. Aminah was too pregnant to flee, and yet staying behind could mean her death.

"She had barely heard of the king of Yemen, whose name was Abrahah al-Ashram. You know the insolent vanity of those people. Paradise begins when you cross the border into their green land. Abrahah despised Mecca for one thing—the Kaaba and the wealth it brought us. Why shouldn't hordes of pilgrims come to his kingdom instead of this wretched desert town? In a dream he saw the solution. He had to build a shrine so grand and luxurious that it would awe any pilgrim who set eyes upon it. He obeyed his dream and called his bejeweled shrine Qullays. If a god had spoken in his ear, Abrahah's ambition might have been realized, but he was listening to demons. They quickly betrayed him. No pilgrims turned away from the Kaaba. The Arabs made up songs ridiculing his gaudy, empty temple. Now Abrahah's vanity turned to anger. He rounded up an army of mercenaries, spear throwers and archers, the scum of the earth, but experienced in war. They began their march on Mecca, and what did our Bedouin brothers do? They greased the way with food and water, sold at a premium. They even provided guides from the hill towns who were jealous of Mecca. Abrahah created wonder with a pack of huge gray monsters, as the ignorant called them. They had never seen drawings of elephants."

I stopped my story and looked at Muhammad. "You think this is only a tale, but the future depends on what I'm saying."

He quietly asked me to go on.

"When word spread that Abrahah's army was only a few miles away, the Quraysh gathered in council. The invader sent word that he would kill no innocent civilians. His wish was to enter the city, raze the Kaaba to the ground, and depart. The emissary who brought this news was lucky he wasn't beheaded on the spot. The Quraysh became furious and vowed to defend Mecca to the last man. One elder dissented, though. 'We can rebuild even the most sacred building,' he argued. 'But if we die, there will be no one left to bring the Kaaba back.'

"That lone voice was your grandfather, Abdul Muttalib. The invaders had scoured the hills to steal our animals, and he had lost the most, more than a hundred camels. If Muttalib could keep his head in the face of such a crime, he was the man to send to the enemy camp as ambassador. Muttalib went and bowed before Abrahah, although obeisance stuck in his throat like a mouthful of thorns. To him he said, 'Sire, withdraw from our home. We cannot fight you, but our idols are not under our control. I cannot vouch for what they might do. Accept tribute from us instead.' Muttalib offered money and fruit from the best orchards to be paid in perpetuity. Abrahah sneered at tribute, which he saw as a sign of weakness."

"Like a true Arab," Muhammad interrupted.

"No, that's the cruelest part. He was an Abyssinian, a foreigner. Yemen had fallen to their king. In those days the demon Christ seduced Abyssinia, and his hand was guiding everything."

"From what I've heard, Christ doesn't inspire war," said Muhammad mildly.

I grew irritated. Why did he refuse to see?

"Christ inspires whatever makes him more powerful. He's no different from any other god," I said glancing at the wine jug. I resisted temptation, as persuasion deserts a loose tongue.

"Muttalib returned to Mecca with the bad news. He counseled calm. He repeated Abrahah's promise not to harm the populace, but panic spread without check like a contagion. Whole streets were abandoned overnight and became prey to wandering ghosts and thieves. The tribal elders held no sway. They fled faster than anyone. Now came the decisive moment."

I paused so that Muhammad would be slightly uneasy, uncertain what I was really about. He knows my reputation for canniness and power brokering. Nothing I do or say is casual.

I let anticipation hang in the air. Then I said, "On the night before the invader reached our gates, I spied on your grandfather."

"Why?" Muhammad was obviously caught off guard.

"Because the Kaaba meant more to his clan than to anyone else. Without the idols, what would happen to the sale of their precious water and the money it brought? Muttalib had done his best to get his family to safety. The only one he couldn't persuade was Aminah, and her peril gave him added incentive. I followed him from his courtyard to the doors of the Kaaba. He seized the handles with both hands and began to wail. He wailed to every god he could think of. He invoked the one God, Allah, but he didn't exclude even the most insignificant idol made of cracked plaster. When he was finished, he composed himself. From the shadows I couldn't hear what he muttered to himself, but we were both Arabs. He left the rest to fate."

I raised my eyebrows. "Can you believe that his prayers were answered?

"That very day a sickness fell over Abrahah's army. Soldiers broke out in sores that oozed poison. Some say a swarm of biting insects swooped down on their camp, but I saw with my own eyes. Within hours the troops began falling to the ground. A day later they were dying in piles. I sneaked beyond the city walls and spied on them. There were no insects. An invisible curse felled them. The war elephants with brass balls on their tusks stood around listlessly, unable to move. Like a man caught in a nightmare, Abrahah realized that the predator had become the prey. The tribes would sniff out this calamity and descend to devour him. He turned tail and ordered an immediate retreat. Suddenly the demon army and its monsters vanished like a mirage."

"I have listened," said Muhammad, "but there is a tale within the tale. Why is this about me?"

"Be patient. Your grandfather, Muttalib, was over-joyed, and his prestige soared. Drunken celebrations clogged the streets. Rich men slept with all their wives and woke up exhausted the next morning. Muttalib remained sober. He called a council to create ways to prevent such a threat from ever happening again. Laws were passed forbidding Jews and Christians from living in Mecca. A street patrol was formed, and armed men guarded the prosperous neighborhoods."

"The guardians, which you lead," said Muhammad quietly.

I smiled and extended an arm. "I'm not threatening you."

"Then why does it feel that way?" he asked.

"Listen to me. The man who demanded that the Jews and Christians be driven out was your grandfa-ther. His decree rests upon your shoulders."

Muhammad was grim. He had never counted on spies. I knew he consorted with the *hanif.* The old ones like Waraqah were beyond my power. If I hadn't liquored up some half-crazy thugs, Uthman wouldn't have been warned. And yet it was necessary.

I expected Muhammad to react with fear or passion, but not with violence. I had no dagger hidden under my couch for a talk with him. He did surprise me, though.

"Do you know why I called you a rebel?" he asked calmly.

I shook my head.

"Because you lead the revolt against change. The new terrifies you. The danger isn't an invisible curse this time. It's the invisible, period."

I gave a disgusted sigh and reached for the wine jug. There was no reason to hold back now. "You talk like one of them."

"They are us. That's what you don't see. What are you really guarding? Slow rot. I smell it in this room."

His voice was strong and steady. He was willing to utter words that get men killed. Had I underestimated him? I pretended to be unmoved while I recorded everything he said in my mind.

"How are they us?" I asked.

"The Quraysh control this city for one reason. It's not money. My grandfather made and lost a fortune. His sons were left weak and stripped of riches. I was reduced to living like a servant in my uncle's house, the last to be given bread and the first to be beaten when his sons were in a rage. But I know that without Abraham, our father, the Quraysh are nothing. We owe him everything. The water of life springs from him. For years that has meant less and less. What is Abraham without the faith of Abraham? Tell me your answer, and I will join you. If you can't, rot with the rest."

I cannot imagine how he managed this speech without challenging me to a fight. Muhammad's eyes flashed, but his hand remained quietly by his side.

"You are no longer welcome inside my gate," I said with cold formality.

"I obey with sadness," he replied.

A moment later he vanished. I threw my wine cup across the room. It smashed against the wall and dripped purple juice down the plaster. No matter, it was undrinkable, spoiled by the heat. Flies buzzed around my head, attracted by the sickly sweetness of a drunkard's breath. There were too many to swat. I covered myself with a blanket and waited for sleep.

7.

A Wandering Mendicant

Because I wandered in from the desert, nobody knows my name. They call me "the chick," because I sit all day with my mouth open, waiting for people walking by to drop food in. It's a cunning way to beg. Everyone knows who I am, and all of Mecca marvels at how I survive. At times there can be nasty surprises. I'm a decent man, or I would tell you some of the filthy objects street urchins have dropped into my mouth.

Today I'm a beggar, but I have ambitions. I hope to become a fool. People pity fools, and those who don't are at least superstitious about them. The best fools have gone mad over God. They even think they speak with God's voice, but it's all babble. I think about that when I'm curled up in an alley on a cold night. Is it better to be pitied or despised? Those are my two choices.

I don't feel sorry for myself. On feast days and especially weddings it's good to sit with your mouth open as the guests pass by. A few will be feeling merry enough to toss a sweetmeat your way. The last wedding was Muhammad's. Mecca couldn't stop talking about it. A trader in his twenties marrying an old woman. Why did he agree? It wasn't for her beauty. The lady Khadijah is forty. Two rich husbands have died on her. So it had to be for her money. He must have played a close game. The widow is rich enough that she resisted all offers from greedy suitors. Rich enough to be the one who proposed to Muhammad too, not the other way around. No one felt she was stooping beneath her station, though, because Khadijah's purity is impeccable. She was waiting for a pure husband, they say.

And most people were glad that Muhammad was rising. I watched him passing in and out of her gate in the days before the ceremony. Being a beggar, I have a high opinion of him. He's never thrown a pebble down my throat to see if I'd choke and get a bit of a laugh, like some others. One day he struck a filthy boy who was about to drop a ball of dung in my mouth.

Naturally, I expected much from the wedding of a man like that. I arrived at the bride's house a few days early. Mostly women came by, always giggling. I turned my face away. It hurts to see the face a pretty woman makes when she sets eyes on me. Next was a young man in dirty sandals carrying a bolt of fine woolen cloth. I seized his leg and held on tight.

"Let me go," he cried. "You're crazy, not blind. Can't you see I'm only a servant?"

But I didn't let go until he shook his leg and hopped up and down like a nomad bitten by sand fleas. It was funny, really, because he didn't dare drop the bolt of cloth to beat me. After that little prank time hung heavy. I got hungry sitting there with my mouth open, until a large ripe date dropped in. Opening my eyes, I saw Muhammad.

"May Allah give you joy," I murmured, rolling the sweet fruit around on my tongue.

Muhammad was in a rush, but he paused with a curious look on his face. "Does the name of Allah help your begging? I wouldn't think so."

I fawned, hoping for another date. "God shows me who is his son when I am fortunate enough to see one."

"So Allah is just one of your tricks, to see who can be flattered?"

Muhammad didn't say this in an insulting tone. He was smiling and at the same time he pulled another date from his sash, putting this one in my hand. A proper and decent gesture.

I bowed. "I'll tell you my secret, sir. I speak of Allah, because I am practicing to be a fool. When fools speak of God, people are more likely to be superstitious about them." Muhammad shook his head with amused wonder and went on his way.

If I heard the tinkle of ankle bells but no giggling, it was usually Khadijah herself bustling past me on her way somewhere. She is always in motion. A rich woman must work twice as hard as a man to keep thieves from her hoard. In summer her caravans are headed for Syria, in winter for Yemen. She paces around the camels at dawn, inspecting every bale and sack. But Khadijah isn't pinch-faced and shrewd, if that's what you think. She wraps her head in black to go out at night, and many a poor wretch cowering from the cold and damp has felt her hand on his shoulder. She brings soup and a cloak, even to strangers. She busies herself behind the scenes to marry off her poor relations and drops gold in their dowries, so that the girls won't wind up with a crook-backed bully no respectable woman would touch.

When she passes me, I murmur *ameerat,* or "princess." Khadijah smiles. She's heard that kind of flattery all her life. More than most, she actually deserves it.

One thing about her is resented, though. When feast days come and the other women observe the tradition of running around the Kaaba, she closes her shutters and stays home. The Hajj is not for her, and Khadijah has enough money that she can make no bones about it. Behind closed doors, say the gossips, she doesn't fondle Muhammad's beard. They sit together and mock the idols. Who knows what trouble it may get them into one day.

As the wedding drew near, the groom's visits became more frequent. Sometimes he was too preoccupied to notice me, but if he did, he had a scrap or two to spare. One morning he caught me hobbling to my place by the gate.

"How did you become lame?" he asked.

"My toes were bitten off by dogs," I said.

"Show me."

I peeled the rags off my feet and let him see the ragged row of toes and stumps where curs had chewed on me.

"Is your pain severe?" he asked.

"Not enough to make me kill myself, but too much to laugh all day," I replied.

Our eyes met. He could see that I wasn't whining to cadge a bit of bread, and I could see that he was actually interested. I wasn't lying at all. My mother made a bad marriage to a drunkard. To make matters worse, her mother-in-law hated her. One day I was left in her charge when I was still a baby in swaddling clothes. Out of contempt, my grandmother left me under a tree while she went to the town well for water. This wasn't in Mecca, but in one of the hill towns surrounding it, on the edge of the wilderness. My grandmother knew very well that packs of wild dogs roam at will, making so brave as to wander into town. Two of them found me under the tree and began to gnaw at my feet, which were sticking out of my bundled clothes. My screams brought a man running, and with a stick he beat the dogs off, but not before they had taken a few toes from each foot. They say when my grandmother returned, she didn't wail. Out of spite, it cost her nothing to see me maimed. Not that I remember anything about it. But one imagines.

You should not suppose that Khadijah spotted Muhammad in the marketplace and felt herself swoon. Nor did he leave love poems pinned to her shutters comparing her almond eyes to a fawn in the moonlight. They were both sober people. She knew two things about Muhammad that anyone in business would be intrigued by. First, he was not all that experienced, having left Mecca on small caravans such as his uncle, Abu Talib, could afford. Second, he could be trusted.

Once the Arabs pin a name on you, it travels with you the rest of your life. I will always be "the chick," and Muhammad expects always to be Al-Amin, the one you can trust.

Khadijah sent her steward Maysarah to greet Muhammad and formally make him an offer. He was to oversee one of her caravans to Syria, and in return the lady would pay him twice the commission she usually offered. You'd think that Al-Amin, the "trustworthy one," wouldn't need such an extravagant bribe, but Khadijah understood that a woman must be prepared to pay enough to discourage thieving from her agents.

The caravan came and went. The steward Maysarah was sent to keep track of the trades and balance the books, but he was also part family spy. Having been with Khadijah since her father and mother died, he had his mistress's ear, and over the years Maysarah had never betrayed her. When he came home with glowing words about Muhammad's character, Khadijah broke her vow never to marry. Passion didn't carry her away. She waited some months. She continued to line Muhammad's pockets. He rose in her esteem, and one day she sent a messenger, her intimate friend Nufaysah, who touched Muhammad's hem with her forehead as if he was the master, offering Khadijah in marriage. A flurry of negotiations started. Uncles got involved, haggling over details like men with a thousand camels to lose or gain. Two clans, the Hashim and the Asad, came together on the suitability of the match, and thus it was.

That's the story as I heard it from servants who squat in the courtyards and gossip with other servants.

Does a woman's heart melt over balanced accounts and good behavior? You know the answer as well as I do.

It would have been auspicious for rain to fall on the wedding day, but it dawned bright and hot like every other day. The first to arrive were young male cousins, loose and wild. Being without women, it suited their mood to kick me, as if to prove that someone in this world was more miserable than they. I closed my mouth when they passed, just to be safe.

But I was also sunk in thought. I must find special words for the groom when he came in procession. It served me well to impress him; he was about to be rich. I kept turning over the same question in my mind. *What would a fool say?* For Muhammad, the best tactic was to babble about God, since I knew he had a weakness there. The crowd was growing thicker now. Like civets, the guests left a perfumed trail behind them as they entered the bride's house. Rich robes swirled in the light wind. The richest women had seed pearls dangling from their gauzy veils. Someone dropped a coin in my mouth, and when I looked closely, it appeared to be silver.

At last Muhammad arrived. He smiled to the left and right, but his eyes looked pensive. He shuffled his feet the way he always did, not lifting them high to protect his new sandals from the dust. When he came abreast of me, a dozen hands were reaching for him. I didn't raise my voice, but quietly said, "Lucky is the man who marries God today."

I was in luck. He noticed me and looked down. "I marry a good woman today, not God," he said.

"She might as well be a bad woman," I said. "Allah is in all creatures."

Guests who were close enough to overhear us began to mutter angrily. I was taking a risk if I kept talking such blasphemous nonsense.

"Your sons will be sons of God, even if they turn out to be drunks and cheats. Do you believe me?" I said.

"I do," said Muhammad, which caused gasps around him.

"Then you are a bigger fool than I am," I said.

"Why?"

"Because all words about God are lies. The Infinite is beyond words."

A few feet reached out to kick me, but not Muhammad's. He didn't smile or frown, but only betrayed sadness with his eyes. Murmuring softly to himself, he tossed me a coin and entered Khadijah's house. A burst of laughter and applause greeted him inside. One Qurayshi came very late, an old man without companions. I was surprised to see Waraqah. His weakness for God is worse than Muhammad's. It has lost him most of his respectability.

"Allah has truly blessed this house," I said, rising on my knees as he rushed through the gate.

Waraqah grimaced. "Forget your tricks. I'm the bride's cousin. I have to be here."

"For the joy of the occasion," I murmured, to get back at him. Everyone knew that old Waraqah hated leaving his house and the mystical studies that devoured his days and ruined his eyes.

"Joy is the fruit of wine," said Waraqah. "I have no use for it. She wants to talk business after the ceremony."

With that, he rushed inside. Don't be amazed that a rich man would waste so many words on a beggar. Waraqah's God loves all men, which shows you how far this religious fever might spread.

TWO

The Angel's Embrace

8.

Khadijah,
the Prophet's Wife

We had no idea. There should have been omens. There were none. God is as unexpected as lightning in the desert. Before he strikes, the sky is as blue as on any other day.

Muhammad and I had been married in peace for fifteen years under that sky. It was a household of women, four daughters and a wife. There were apricots soaked in rose water on the shelf. When a caravan came home from Syria, each of our girls got a precious little bell to hang around her ankle. When my girls walked, a silvery tinkling brightened the path before them.

Muhammad could have acted like a king behind these walls, or a beast. It was common enough. But I had watched him closely before I unfolded my heart's desire. I wasn't born a fool. He wasn't the only young man who listened to the poets in the bazaar and sat in the shade on sweltering days talking with his cousins. People ridiculed me for offering myself to such a young man. "It's like buying a camel and refusing to tie it up," they said. "It's in an animal's nature to stray." My money ensured that none of them laughed to my face, though. I didn't care that Muhammad had asked his uncle, Abu Talib, for his daughter's hand. The girl was sleek as a cat with eyes as soft as a deer's. Old Talib refused him, because he had set his sights on a better marriage with one from the Makhzum clan.

When Muhammad was new and shy with me, he nervously confessed this failed proposal. I burst out laughing. "Not at you," I said, seeing his crestfallen look. "My first two husbands came from the Makhzum clan. They left me twice rich. Is that revenge enough for you?"

He paused, weighing his words. "You will lift me far above any life I've ever known. My grandfather Muttalib was the last elder in my clan to hold sway. I'm a wanderer among men. I listen to songs, but cannot sing. I hear the poets, but cannot read what they say or write better words if I could think of them, which I can't."

He was surprised when I shrugged this off. "Two kinds of people can't read, the illiterate and royalty.

We'll just pretend you're a king. My foreman will read for you."

If Muhammad had turned into a tyrant after we married, I would have had only myself to blame. No one in Mecca saw what we did the day before the wedding. They would not have believed it. We bartered over our future. Well, I did.

"How do you intend to treat me?" I asked.

"How would you like to be treated?" he said. Caution. I like that in a man. He smiled. "They call you a princess, but I was born too low to be any good as a courtier."

"Treat me like a beautiful young girl," I said. "But never let me guess what you really think."

"That is what I really think," he said, as soberly as if he were assessing the weight of a Byzantine gold piece.

We were lying on a couch—not touching—with the shutters closed and all the servants ordered from the house. It does no good to hide behind doors. They always eavesdrop, just as they always steal from the olive jar and pretend that yesterday's lamb has gone bad.

I remembered how I looked in the mirror that morning. I said, "Never be tempted by other women. Betrayal would shame me, and shame would kill me."

Without thinking, my fingers traced a wrinkle around my eyes, still a shallow wrinkle. Before long it would be a crease.

"There's no reason to be afraid. I am betrayed every day. I know shame," Muhammad said.

I couldn't hide my surprise. "Who betrays you?"

"My tongue, which is why I rarely speak." Muhammad meant his accent, which, to tell the truth, everyone notices. He spent too much time with the Bedouin because of his timid mother, who postponed the day he would have to breathe filthy city air. Twenty years later, he sounds faintly as if he just stepped out of a sheep enclosure in the hills. We were comfortable together, lying there, each lost in a dream of what this marriage would be like. His accent was charming to me.

Finally, and with a blush I didn't know I possessed, I said, "Don't reveal any other women you've been with. But I have to know that you aren't sick." If I had picked the right suitor, he had to be pure.

"But I am sick. Some days I think it's fatal."

Muhammad rose and walked to the window, peering through the cracks in the shutter. His face was streaked with light and shade, like the image of a zebra my father brought back from Abyssinia when I was a girl.

"Mecca is my sickness," he murmured. "I get infected again every day. Sometimes with fear, sometimes with rage. On the streets I see the walking dead, and my clan, the Hashim, are almost beggars. I may never recover." He turned around and saw my mystified look. "As for my body, it has no weaknesses. You could store wine in my belly and load my back with saddle bags like a camel."

An Arab cannot consider himself respectable unless he has skill in lying. Our life is haggling. We barter to stay one step ahead of drought, famine, and the malicious gods. This back-and-forth with my fine young Muhammad could have been the prelude to disaster. I knew that it wasn't. Not from woman's intuition. I knew because Muhammad passed my tests. He asked nothing for himself. He didn't insinuate that I should pity him for being an orphan. He didn't sit in profile so I could admire his curved nose or carelessly dangle a curl over his forehead. Not that a woman doesn't notice.

Even so, I hesitated. My father taught me a saying: "A chameleon doesn't leave one tree until he is sure of the next." I had the cook put rare dishes on the table— roast duck bathed in pomegranate syrup, deep-sea fish so delicate that the skin glistened like a rainbow. I did this to see if he salivated. A poor man cannot help but drool, and if he drools over a duck, how secretly he must be drooling over my money. Muhammad's eyes didn't even wander to the food. He kept his gaze on me. A woman can resist anything but attention.

It wouldn't surprise me to know that Allah watched our every move, heard our every word. They were probably his words in some way, fated and sealed. All my life, I assumed that my will was mine. I had more strength than ten other women. I was called "princess," not "surrender." It's a shock to realize that all this time my will was God's.

It was his will that our two baby boys died in the cradle. I awoke one morning before dawn. It wasn't the hour when a baby usually cries. On that morning, when the first boy died, the silence in the house was different, as if the angel of death had whispered overhead. I couldn't bring myself to run into the baby's room, but sent a servant. And the second time? I had a dream of a boy running after a flock of sheep in the mountains. He looked down at his feet as he ran, and he saw the shadow of a wolf. Before he could cry out, I awoke.

Muhammad didn't want any women to wail over our babies after they died; he forbade mourners in the house. When I asked him why, he said, "If an orphan can't handle grief alone, he won't survive." Rarely did he speak of his past that way. No matter how deep into his eyes I gazed, I never saw scars on his heart. Strange, given that this life is made of scars.

But it wasn't in me to wail, either. I had married off three grown children before I ever met Muhammad. My new babies were precious, but if one died, a part of me wasn't ripped away. I kept this a secret, but Muhammad sensed it. He was unhappy when I ordered two animals to be sacrificed in the Kaaba. It was considered only prudent to appease the gods after any kind of misfortune. I was dressing in a black veil when he appeared at the bedroom door, tight-lipped. His face was pale.

"Are you going? You don't have to," he said. I told him that I couldn't leave something like this to servants.

"And which gods do you think will help us?" he asked. He ticked off the names of Hubal, Al-Lat, Manat, and Al-Uzza. In Mecca everyone sacrifices to them, even those who have doubts. We're practical. It costs little enough to please the idols.

"I don't know which one. All of them," I said. I tried to sound casual as I smeared an extra layer of kohl around my eyes as a sign of grief. But I felt guilty pretending to be a believer. Who knows? Maybe one of the gods cursed our babies, or us. These things are impossible to fathom. I watched Muhammad standing behind me in the little polished mirror.

"You can forbid me to go," I said.

In a sarcastic voice that he rarely used, he said, "Can a husband pretend to be more powerful than all the gods? Go if you must."

I went. It wasn't piety that drove me, but fear and grief. I didn't want the gods' disfavor. But I didn't want their protection either, the way common, superstitious people do. If I had dragged ten terrified animals to the altar and watched their throats being slit, would that have saved my two babies? What I wanted was to have the knife in my heart come out. Although I kept my desperation quiet, I had to find relief. If the gods existed—if only one existed—maybe it had the power to grant mercy to one in pain. The sacrifice was made, with many citizens standing around and nodding their approval.

When I came home, Muhammad asked me if I felt better. I shook my head. I felt ashamed to put on such a dumb show before gawkers and idlers, people whose only interest was in seeing a rich woman suffer despite her money.

I've never pretended to have humility, but my pride didn't stop me from running to Muhammad and begging his forgiveness. He lifted up my face and asked me to look at him. Then he said, "I understand your despair. Bring it to me. Half your pain comes from keeping it a secret."

I can't say that the knife immediately withdrew from my heart just because I had a kind husband. That took many months. But my husband and I sat up the rest of the night talking between us about things that wives rarely speak about, such as our sense of frailty. When we stand so low in creation, as every girl is taught, our hope is that at least the gods will give us strength. I was such a girl, wondering where protection would come from in a violent world.

Giving birth is a death sentence for one mother in six, maybe more. I'm willing to believe, but in what? The finger of fate passes over the scrolls and chooses this one for pain, that one for delight, this one for life, that one for death. Has this invisible hand ever been seen by anyone, even the most devout? Once seen, would it change just because a pitiful suffering woman cries out? Fate wipes out creatures by the thousands with a single flash flood in the hills or a summer of drought. We humans are creatures too, subject to the same whimsical catastrophes.

This episode of the sacrifice could have caused Muhammad to condemn me; instead, it brought us closer. We found that we shared no brilliant answers. We shared the same questions instead, and that was enough.

It was my custom to go to the bazaar every morning to inspect the goods and keep an eye on prices.

Once I got married there was no practical need for me to do this. I had turned all my business affairs over to Muhammad. He resisted at first. "There is no need. You've run your own affairs for years," he argued. "And if it's my pride you're worried about, don't."

"It's the pride of every other man I'm worried about," I said. They could barely endure taking orders from a woman. I didn't want them whispering behind Muhammad's back that I married him just so I could emasculate him.

I won't say the matter was settled in one conversation. It's always delicate when a poor man is yoked to a rich woman. Muhammad understood. When a big ox and a small ox try to pull a cart together, it will likely tip over. I told my old steward, Maysarah, to present all the accounts to my husband from now on. He raised an eyebrow, but obeyed. So you see, I could have spent the rest of my life behind doors driving the servants crazy, the way respectable women do. I tried. After two weeks Muhammad begged me, for my own sanity and everyone else's, to keep up my customary ways. The caravan camps were my natural habitat. As he put it, I would still be a lady even if my sandals smelled of camel dung. Unlike the chameleon, I jumped to a new tree, but kept one foot on the old one.

I went on my inspections even when I was with child. The first delivery was two months away when an old man called out to me, "So it's true. You really did change your sex."

It was Waraqah, who had only grown stranger as he grew older. He was sitting on a low wall in the warm winter sun. My legs were sore from waddling down the cobbled street, and I decided to have a rest beside him.

"Ah," he said. "You've given up a man's life, but you're still as brave as a man."

"Let people talk. I don't have to be brave to sit beside you," I said. "Unless I've made a mistake and you still have a tooth left in your head."

He tilted his head back and gave a croaking laugh. "I'm not the one who will bite you if you're seen with me. There are others who will be happy to do it."

He was only half joking. The rich old man was regarded with suspicion among the elders. Waraqah no longer sat with them in the inns, and he hadn't made things any easier for himself by hanging around the Kaaba, muttering oaths at the pilgrims who passed nearby.

I said, "You don't fool me, you know." The veins in my legs had stopped throbbing. I balanced myself on the wall so that my swollen belly didn't make my back ache so much. "You're not as cracked as they say."

Waraqah shot me a sidelong glance. "If I'm not cracked, then what am I?"

I searched my mind, but he didn't wait for a reply. "The word you're looking for is subversive. I'm a snake in a basket of dates. Like your husband."

The expression on my face made him give out another croaking laugh. "You've made him rich, and you did it overnight. But a dangerous mind doesn't get less dangerous swathed in finery."

I was struck silent, which seemed to please Waraqah. The penalty for free thinking had gotten severe during the past few years. Mecca was no longer the city I grew up in. We breathed suspicion. Muhammad wanted to keep his good name, but he would no longer be Al-Amin, the trusted one, if people couldn't trust his opinions. For most men, words are the same as thoughts. As soon as a thought is in their head, it's on their tongue. My husband had thoughts he didn't speak.

The change that came over the city happened almost the day that the gates slammed shut behind Abrahah and his army. It wasn't enough that the invaders all fell sick and their war elephants retreated like a mirage in the desert. Mecca felt defenseless as never before. A foreigner had breached the one barricade we thought was impassable, the desert. Now the Qurayshi elders decreed that no Christian or Jew should set foot inside

Mecca. Since the idols had saved the city by miraculously defeating the invaders, they should have no competition. Foreign gods were banned, and worshiping them meant death or exile. One of Muhammad's own cousins was exposed as a *hanif* who bowed to one God and was forced to flee. The *hanif* were no more to be seen, except for Waraqah, and he had grown much quieter.

The rights of Jews and Christians meant nothing. To ordinary people only their money did. If a Jew was so rich that his business couldn't be done without him, he could pay a levy to come within the city walls. Once here, he couldn't be seen praying or doing obeisance to his god, Yahweh.

The Quraysh had risen to such power that they were able to enforce these decrees. Abu Talib listened to Muhammad's pleas for tolerance. Waraqah muttered at the door of the Kaaba. They were powerless to intervene, however, when the whole tribe stood against them. "I've tried to wear them down," Abu Talib said mournfully. "My words evaporated like a summer shower hitting a hot stone wall."

The rabble were organized into gangs who roamed the alleys beating on drunks and frightening servant girls on their way to the well with water jugs. A hush settled over the city. If you clamp down, people will obey, and the obedient can be mistaken for the contented, if you squint hard enough. To hear the elders talk about it, the Year of the Elephant, as everyone started to call it, became the beginning of a golden age.

This state of Mecca went through my mind as I sat beside Waraqah. "Get pregnant. Drop as many young as you want," he said. "But deep down you're with us."

I looked at the ground, pressing my fingers into my upper thigh to make the biggest blue vein stop bulging.

"So I'm not far wrong," he muttered, interpreting my silence. "I can tell you something else. Muhammad broke my heart when he left the cause. There were only four *hanif* to stand up for the truth, and we were all growing old. I think of your husband every day, but we barely speak when our paths cross. Maybe now I have an understanding with you."

"Perhaps."

It was Waraqah's turn to look surprised. "What gives a woman this kind of courage? I was just goading you."

I shrugged. It wasn't courage, though. My caravans have traveled the length of the Arab world, from Yemen to Syria. When they returned home, I sat my men down and made them tell me about what they saw and heard. My father didn't raise me to be ignorant. Like Muhammad, he was fond of the old sayings. One of them is this: "A fat woman is better in winter than a blanket." My father would frown and say to me, "I want you to be more than a better blanket when you grow up."

My men told me in particular how foreigners think, because when you know what is in a customer's mind, you have an advantage over him. That's how it began. After a while, though, the peculiarity of men's minds gained its own fascination. Arabs believe that Abraham built the Kaaba, but Jews believe he founded their tribe in Jerusalem. We say that God ordered Abraham to sacrifice his older son, Ishmael. The Jews say it was his younger son, Isaac. Muhammad was a bit shocked that I knew such things, perhaps more shocked that they made me think skeptical thoughts about the idols surrounding the Kaaba. He quickly realized, however, that this was a bond between us. We rarely spoke about it.

"I don't mind being hated, you know," said Waraqah out of the blue. "A thousand curses never tore a shirt."

I smiled. That was another of my father's sayings. The old man and I were relaxed now. He pointed to a donkey some yards away. The animal was tied to a long stick attached to a grinding stone. He trudged in slow circles, and as he did a lazy-looking boy threw grain under the millstone to be ground into coarse flour.

"There is your common Arab," said Waraqah. "He walks in circles and thinks he's getting somewhere. Tie an idol to his nose, and he thinks the gods are leading the way to Paradise."

The old man was growing deaf, and he said these words in a voice loud enough that two merchants passing by overheard him. They looked our way and frowned. Then seeing who it was, they bowed and moved on quickly.

I got up and dusted off my skirts, which were speckled with chaff from the millstone. "You know people who were driven out of Mecca," I said. "They talked the way you do."

"They didn't see what's coming. I've read the signs. I can afford to wait."

With this strange comment Waraqah waved me on my way, saying that we'd meet again. When I returned home, I told Muhammad everything. I didn't leave out that he had broken Waraqah's heart. He winced but said nothing, and when I asked him to open his mind to me, my husband said, "Better a free dog than a caged lion." Men. They could pass their whole lives with old sayings. And yet I knew that my encounter struck deep inside him.

9.

Jafar,
a Son of Abu Talib

It finally happened. A *jinn* has driven Muhammad mad. He was seized in the hills somewhere, inside a cave, they say. Why was he there in the first place? It is well known that *jinns* hole up in caves, and the wind that blows through the blackness is their howling. Even shepherd boys won't chase a lost lamb into a cave without making a cut in their forearm and offering drops of blood to the gods.

A stranger in the street told me what had happened, which meant that the news was spreading fast. I ran to Muhammad's house near the center of town. Who would I meet there? My family is Hashim, and our first instinct would be to gather the clan around any member who's in trouble. But trouble isn't the same as being seized by a demon. That kind of thing is infectious.

It was just as likely that I'd run into spies sent by the Qurayshi elders. I wouldn't put it past them to use this as a pretext for seizing control of Muhammad's affairs. Anything to get close to his wife's money.

There were no spies and no Hashim men milling around, though. There was nobody at all. A stray dog was sniffing at the locked gate. I stood there, listening. In a house of women there's always something going on. Gossip, clattering pots, the clack of a loom. Here, there was nothing. I considered pounding on the gate and shouting for somebody to come. I was quite anxious for him. I would beg his wife to bring in a priest or a worker in spells. I looked around. The houses are pressed close together near the Kaaba, and my shouts would be overheard. Reluctantly I walked away. I wasn't an elder, and feeble as the Hashim have become, it's the elders' business to help or condemn one of their own. Let it never be said that I was the first to move against him by raising an alarm.

I fretted all the way home. Muhammad has strange ways. Everyone knows that, not least his family. I heard that he and some others, including his oldest friend, Abu Bakr, had gathered by night to swear an oath. A secret ceremony? I hate the *hanif,* but to tell you the truth, that sounded promising. My cousin is too sober for his own good. The spice of intrigue wouldn't hurt.

Once the oath was made public, I ran to Muhammad in disgust.

"What is this? You've sworn to give to the poor? What the gods won't do, you are going to do instead?"

It was ridiculous. I'm not yet forty, but I agree with the old ones who grumble that this kind of sacrilege will tear society apart. Muhammad listened to me ranting for a few minutes, saying nothing. His silence made me more agitated.

"You think a man's life should be about helping dirty, squalid slaves?" I cried.

"I don't know what a man's life should be about. That's precisely why I help dirty, squalid slaves," he replied calmly. "Do you have a few you can spare?"

Muhammad became even stranger after his marriage. I, his favorite cousin, no longer could tap at his window to run off on an adventure. No one ever supposed he would lose his mind. I ached for news that he was all right. Muhammad wouldn't leave his house, but gossip can pass through the tiniest crack in a fortress. Soon servants ran from the house of Abu Bakr to see what my father was willing to pay for scraps of news. They were excited, out of breath. Abu Talib was taking a nap as usual, so I met them. I sat them down and gave out dates and well water. I saw them furtively slip the fruit into their robes rather than eat it.

"Tell me, quick," I demanded. "If you're spreading scandal, I'll have you whipped."

The youngest one, a curly-haired Syrian who was good-looking and therefore presentable among people of quality, spoke up. "He was wandering in the hills by himself. Very dangerous. Some people don't never return, and those people had ideas, just like him."

"What do you know about ideas?" I asked angrily.

The Syrian slave gave me an insolent stare, and my hand itched to take out the leather crop I keep under my robe. But I let him proceed.

"I know about *tahannuf*," he said. "My master has gone on such a one. He thinks he goes into the hills by himself, but I am sent along to keep guard. Out of sight, you can bet. He wouldn't like it."

Well, it's no crime to go on *tahannuf.* For as long as we can remember, Arabs have sought solace in the wilderness. The meadows outside Mecca are ideal for this—green and quiet, closer to heaven. As for myself, I help to make sure Mecca stays filthy, if you know what I mean. But the Syrian's master, Abu Bakr, took *tahannuf* every spring, and so did Muhammad. Muhammad's interest in business affairs had steadily waned, year by year. Even his four daughters found him aloof; he had turned away from our world, vainly hoping to find another.

"What are you telling me? Nothing new," I said. I reminded this insolent slave of an old saying: "A grateful dog is worth more than an ungrateful man." To underline the point, I held out a small coin. Despite himself, his eyes widened greedily.

He said, "I'm telling you, great sir, I have seen men kidnapped when they go on such retreats. I've hidden behind rocks and watched their throats get cut and their bodies flung into gullies. Some of them still had money in their purses."

"They didn't have money for long," I said dryly. "You can vouch for that, can't you?"

The ambushes couldn't be denied. Who goes on *tahannuf* but the devout? And no one is more devout than these troublemakers who cry out against our sacred ways. Some of them go into the hills to find their God, and we make sure they do. It serves as a warning to the rest. Muhammad had more sense.

"So you were sent in secret to spy on Muhammad?" I asked.

"To protect him, great sir, not to spy."

"Abu Bakr had reason to fear for his friend's life?"

The Syrian slave bit his tongue; it wasn't his place to divulge his master's intentions. He looked surprised when I put the coin in his palm and closed his hand around it. "You did well," I murmured. I love

Muhammad. Once my father took him in as an orphan, he became my brother. In a tolerant voice I asked the slave to spare no details. He had to tell me what he saw that made Muhammad lose his mind.

"For a long time, he did nothing out of the ordinary," the slave began. "Master Muhammad liked to walk on the slopes of Mount Hira, because it lies only an hour by foot from the city walls. I got bored following him. It didn't come into my head that he was searching for something, a hideaway, like. One day he found a lonely cave whose mouth was hidden by brush. He cleaned the cave of all the nasty debris and animal skeletons, even washing the floor himself with rags dipped in a stream. He began to take long retreats inside the cave, sometimes from dawn to nightfall. There were times when he had to use the stars to guide his way home. Like I told you, I was bored something terrible. I became restless sitting down below on the hillside with nothing to do but wait for him to leave. What use is there in avoiding other people like that? A rich man should enjoy himself. He should spread his money wherever he can find wine and women."

The slave thought he was playing to my nature, but I showed no reaction. He went on.

"Master Muhammad's trips to the cave started coming more often. One day I couldn't help myself. I fell asleep in the sun, and when I opened my eyes,

Muhammad was standing over me. He smiled a secret smile, but spoke not a word. We two made our way down the mountain together. That didn't stop my master. He insisted I keep watch even if Muhammad had caught on."

"Listen carefully," I said. "Did you see any signs?"

"Of madness? No, great sir."

"Signs of anything unusual?"

I put my question cautiously. It seemed impossible that Muhammad was casting spells or trying to lure *jinns* to help him with some dark business. He wasn't capable of such things (although I know more than a few who are).

The Syrian thought for a moment before replying. "He had moods. Of that I'm sure."

"What kind of moods? I thought you hung back, hiding from him?" I queried.

"At first. But once he caught on to me, we kept company. He wanted to talk." The slave's voice was hesitant. People of quality share their lives with servants. There's no other choice. We're surrounded by them day and night, but there's a barrier between us. The slave would be doing Muhammad no good by saying that he had lowered that barrier.

Do you want proof of how anxious I was? I went into the pantry and brought out the best bread and cold lamb. Without a word I spread the victuals out on the table. The slave watched warily. I tore off a piece of flatbread, wrapped it around a morsel of meat, and handed it to him. I was willing to lower the barrier that far to get more news, but the look in my eyes warned the Syrian not to push me. I knew I should have called the slave by his name, but I forgot to ask. I doubted that I would ever see him again.

"It's dry," he mumbled as he chewed. The cheeky bastard wanted me to bring out some wine. I ignored him. When he had swallowed, I told him to finish his story.

He said, "Muhammad and me talked almost every day coming down the mountain. He liked to ask me questions."

I couldn't hide my surprise. "What kind of questions?"

"It depended on his mood. That's what I'm trying to tell you." The slave eyed the lamb. I gave a curt nod, and he took another chunk, holding it in his fist until he satisfied what I wanted to know. "One day we saw a dead kid goat in a ditch. It had fallen in and broken its leg. The dogs got to it before anyone heard it. Muhammad stood a long time staring at the gnawed carcass. 'Where is that goat now?' he muttered. I assumed he was talking to himself, so I didn't respond. He looked over at me and said, 'I lost two sons before they even knew they had a father. I lost my father before he knew he had a son. Where are they now?'

"I was nervous, but I spoke up. 'Wherever they were,' I said, 'it was different from where dead goats go.' He laughed and said, 'A good answer, but it wriggles out of the question.' After that he was quiet all the rest of the way home."

I held up my hand for him to stop talking. I needed a moment to think. Muhammad never mourned his lost sons properly before the gods. Word started going around that he was a secret unbeliever. Because the Hashim clan was too weak, Abu Talib, my father, couldn't send anyone out to punish those who talked against Muhammad. We had to swallow our pride and take it. But if this Syrian was to be believed, the thought of those two dead babies preyed on him. *Jinns* sniff out weakness of mind; they know how to twist the knot of self-torment inside a man.

"Did he talk about his dead sons again?" I asked. The slave shook his head. "Did he ever bring his new son to the cave?" The slave shook his head again.

This new son was another piece of strange business. Muhammad is forty this year, but his wife, who is fifteen years older, cannot give him more children. He gave no sign that this was a grief for him. Then one day he came home and said, "I want you to buy me a son."

Khadijah was all but speechless. "Who?" she asked, keeping her wits about her.

Muhammad explained that he was wandering through the bazaar when his eyes fell upon a young boy being sold as a slave. A raiding party had just returned to town, with captives taken on the trading routes. These raiders have only one thought in mind, to grab their prey and get away without being killed. They never think to take care of their prizes, so that they can be fit to be sold. Like the others, this boy was starving and gaunt. His eyes were sunken, but when Muhammad stared at him, the boy stared back defiantly. As if he had any power to do anything. But Muhammad was impressed, and he thought of the future.

A woman of Khadijah's age doesn't usually want to discuss what might happen in the future. She agreed to buy the boy for Muhammad. When he was brought to the house, she was just as impressed by him as her husband was. They changed his name from "Zayd, son of who knows what" to "Zayd, son of Muhammad." So now the wealth of a lifetime may be passed on to a foreign captive. One day I may have to fight him for my share.

The Syrian was waiting impatiently for my next question. The only one left was the obvious. "What happened to drive Muhammad mad?"

"*Jinns*," said the slave quickly.

I frowned. "Don't repeat what everyone else is saying. You were there. What did you see?"

The slave trusted me enough to tell the truth. "I saw a man running away from something he can never understand. We were on the mountain, but Master Muhammad didn't come out of the cave at sunset. I didn't know what to do. He has stayed all night before, when it's warm enough. I could run home and sleep in a warm bed, then go back at dawn, and nobody would be the wiser. But I stayed. Ramadan is a strange month, they say. I didn't know what might happen. So I wrapped myself on the ground and tried to sleep. The next thing I knew, Master Muhammad stepped right over me. His heel brushed my shoulder, and I looked up to see him. He was as white as the dead. He acted as if he didn't see me lying there, but just kept walking, at a fast pace. Like I said, he was running from something. I gathered myself and ran after him. He didn't look like a man who was in this world. No matter how loud I called, he wouldn't look back or answer me. We went like that until we got to town. Muhammad stopped in his tracks and stared at the sky. He wasn't staring like some ordinary lunatic, but as if he expected someone to fly down. If we had been inside the walls, people would have gawked, I can tell you. Then he shuddered so hard I could see his body quiver under his thick robes. A few minutes later we went through the gates, and I followed him home until he shut himself up inside."

So, there you are. The worse had come to the worst. I turned my face away. I didn't want the slave to get the satisfaction of seeing the effect his tale had on me. With a wave of the hand I signaled for him to leave. He and the other slaves wasted no time bolting out the door. Abu Bakr would surmise that his trusted Syrian was selling information. I sighed. Tomorrow he would find another rich house and another one willing to fling some coins at him. Muhammad's reputation was dashed. Our enemies were already laughing with glee.

Which is worse, the wickedness of the world or the curse of demons? I sat there pondering the question until the night robbed the room of all light. Muhammad didn't deserve this fate. Or maybe he did. Ill luck befalls any man who thinks he can pry the gods' secrets out of their fists.

10.

Ruqayah,
Muhammad's Third Daughter

His first fear was for himself. For his soul, I mean.
My father knew that something must have gone
horribly wrong. Only later did we discover that he
had run from the cave to the top of the mountain to
hurl himself onto the rocks below. He never suspected
God's wrath. Yet when he summoned the light, it
shattered him. Allah can drive someone as mad as any
demon.

I was showing my littlest sister, Fatimah, who was
barely five, how to pick flowers in the courtyard when
he staggered home. "My child!" he cried, clasping
Fatimah so hard to his breast that she could hardly
breathe. His agitation made me tremble. After a long,
deep stare into Fatimah's eyes, he ran to his room and
bolted the door. I don't think he even recognized me.

We will never forget the seventeenth day of Ramadan. The brunt of it fell on my mother. I watched her pace the floor, growing paler and paler. That first day we lived in dreadful silence. My father allowed no one to approach him. Leaning at his door, we girls heard weeping and loud, tormented cries. I tell you, I had heard the words "gnashing of teeth," but the actual sound, like stones grinding together, is horrifying.

On the second day he allowed my mother into the room. When she emerged again, her face was set and grim. I thought my father must be dying. When I asked her, my mother said, "Some things are worse than dying. There is also death in life."

She wouldn't let me ask any more questions, but sent me to fetch the servants. When they were assembled, my mother put on a face of incredible calm.

"I won't lie to you. The worst may not have happened, but if not, God save us from the worst," she said.

My mother couldn't stop the anxious cries her words caused, but she quickly moved on to allay them. "None of you will have to leave. You are safe with me. You've heard the sounds of your master in torment. If you love him and trust me, listen to my orders."

With that she told the servants to run to our relatives among the Hashim and bring them to her. "Don't give out any details. It's not for you to suggest anything, not with a certain tone of voice or a rolling of the eyes. This is no idle moment. It's a crisis that will tell me everything about who you are from this day forward."

What could they say? My mother's will subdued the servants as long as they were behind our walls. As they ran off to gather the clan, some may have panicked or indulged in wild fantasies. We all did. As soon as the house was empty, my mother took me aside into a private corner with my two older sisters. Fatimah could be distracted by giving her a doll to play with in the next room.

"Your father isn't mad. He has been overwhelmed," she said. "We will nurse him. We will watch over him. Those things go without saying. I know they are the desires of your heart. But only waiting will tell the tale."

"What has overwhelmed him?" asked Zaynab. As the oldest, she had the right to speak first. Later as events unfolded, she was not so faithful to my father. Zaynab's mind was occupied every waking hour with getting a husband. Even at that critical moment, her thoughts lived halfway in another man's house.

"He doesn't have enough of his wits back to make sense," said my mother, who was always candid with us. "He mumbles the word 'power' over and over."

In Arabic she said *qadr.* The only way for me to explain the word to strangers is "power." For us there are hints and shadows in this word. It signifies a mystery, a holy presence that has descended to shatter one's body and mind.

My second sister, Umm Kulthum, stole a glance in my direction. She didn't want to understand anything at first. Her instinct was to protect the young ones. Besides Fatimah, there was the slave boy Zayd. He was new, and we had not learned to think of him as our brother yet. He was some years older than Fatimah, but too young to understand how a grown man in the space of a single night could turn into a quivering heap.

The Hashim men came quickly, demanding in loud voices to set eyes on Muhammad for themselves. My mother refused. "You will see him when he's himself again. What lies in that room is not Muhammad."

An unfortunate choice of words. Mutterings about *jinns* arose. My mother knew they would, but something else was on her mind. She had to keep Muhammad's name from being ruined. Instead of fighting with rumors, she went on the offensive.

"When was the Kaaba in ruins? When was it rebuilt? Let any man step forward who did more to rebuild it than my Muhammad."

The rumbling began to die down. You see, the Hashim were so poor and trampled on that they had little left but their honor. My father was the most honorable among them. He earned that title five years before. The Kaaba had become a shambles. A wag said that it was a good thing pilgrims came for the Hajj to run around the Kaaba, because if they dared to touch it the walls would fall down. As things stood, no one was willing to repair the sagging roof and the cracks that ran from top to bottom. Fate then stepped in. A flash flood stormed through the center of town. The waters dug a course straight for the Kaaba, almost submerging it.

In a panic people ran to save the idols. My mother laughed at that. "They can't wait to rescue the very gods that caused this," she muttered. By the time the waters receded, the roof had collapsed. There was no choice now. A certain faction was still too superstitious to intervene, holding that the walls were sacred, even though they were on the verge of falling down. To touch them risked angering the gods even more.

Others grew disgusted with this attitude. The issue was settled when Al-Mugirah, a rough, sensible type, walked up to the Kaaba in front of everyone with a sledgehammer. He took a swing and knocked a huge gap in one of the walls.

"If the gods want to kill me, let them do it now," he shouted.

Nothing happened, so it was decided to start over and build a shrine that would last forever. All at once the very clans that wanted to kill each other to keep the Kaaba intact vied to make a new one. That too proved futile, for when they got down to the foundations, a layer of green stone was exposed that could not be broken, no matter how many burly slaves knocked at it. The Quraysh declared that the foundation was laid by Abraham and must not be touched.

My father watched quietly off to one side. He came home one night and said, "A fellow brought a bowl of blood to the work site today. He held it up in the air, screaming that his clan was entitled to finish the work, no one else. He was backed up by twenty toughs with knives drawn. Who knows where he got so much blood? It spilled over the edge of the bowl and streaked his face while he screamed."

Yet this bizarre incident made my father's fortune in a strange way. There was one stone set in the eastern wall of the Kaaba that my father told us to hold in reverence. It was black and polished and about the width of a large man's hand. "We are the people of Abraham, and when he built this shrine, he laid in place a single stone from the time of Adam and Eve. In that stone is our hope," he said. I didn't know what my father meant by "our hope," but I can't remember a time when the Black Stone was not touched and bowed before by every pilgrim.

When it came time to set the Black Stone back in place, a feud broke out among the clans. Nobody wanted to grant the privilege to anyone else. At the same time, no one wanted to risk the wrath of the gods by not claiming it for himself. Fights broke out daily at the site, until it was decided that only one man, Muhammad, was trusted enough by all the clans to settle the dispute.

Muhammad wasn't eager to go. I found him lingering by the gate with his best robe on, washing his hands in a basin, then calling for fresh water so he could wash them again.

"It's a sly tactic to call on me," he said. "There is no one who deserves the privilege over anybody else. Whoever I choose, the rest will be furious with me. They will fall on each other's necks, and when the dust clears, our family will be blamed. We will be weaker than ever, which is the whole point."

You wouldn't think that the same man would have returned home two hours later wreathed in smiles. "I did it," he said with quiet exultation. He called for the best sweet wine and even diluted it three times with water so we girls could drink.

"What did you do?" my mother asked, as baffled as anyone.

"I stared solemnly at the rock for a long time, as if it was going to deliver an answer. In fact, I was scouring my brain in mounting desperation. Then the simplest idea occurred to me. I ordered that someone bring a large sheet of cloth. I had the Black Stone placed in the center and signaled for the elders of the four major clans to each take a corner of the sheet. 'Now lift it together to the height where the stone will be placed,' I said. 'Then you will all share in the honor and reap the same reward from the gods.'"

From that moment on my father earned a respectful nod and a raised beaker at the inns. But he insisted to us, his family, that he wasn't wise. "I am only a man among men. The point was to give these hotheads an escape route, so they wouldn't lose face. Nothing more. If the gods noticed, they were as amused as I was."

My mother's efforts to remind the clan of their debt to my father worked to hold off the spiral of ruin momentarily.

Several days later my father appeared at the door of his room. He still looked pale and stunned, but he held his arms out, and one by one his daughters ran into them. When I embraced him, it felt as if half his body had wasted away. The last to be embraced was Fatimah, who was frightened by the deep black circles around my father's eyes.

You could see that he was hurt when Fatimah backed away. "What's wrong, my child?"

"I want my papa back," she blurted out and burst into tears.

My father swept her into his arms, calming Fatimah's fears. Even as he did this, he looked around at the rest of us. His eyes said, "And do you think your papa is not here?"

You must understand, during that terrible week we held the family together by not speaking our deepest fears out loud. I asked to be taken to the Kaaba to pray. I'm sure my sisters did as well. We avoided looking at one another during meals. Some of the servants weakened and began to spread rumors; my mother wasn't above taking a stick to them.

Then as quickly as we lost him, my father became himself again. Like a patient whose fever has broken, he mastered his crisis. I don't know how he did it. Yet one day I found him sitting alone on the floor of the pantry eating one flatbread after another between gobbets of lamb and beakers of well water. When he saw me, he burst out laughing.

"Forgive me, Ruqayah, you shouldn't see your father with a greasy chin and bits of food hanging from his beard. But I am famished!"

"Your chin? Papa, you should see yourself. Your whole face looks like Fatimah's when she's gotten loose in the butter." I laughed with him, even as tears blurred my eyes.

He stuffed himself, and then he slept. By nightfall he called his wife and us daughters into his presence. He smelled freshly bathed, with a touch of rose oil in his hair. His beard was no longer an unruly weed patch, and his eyes gleamed, even though they seemed far away.

"My dear," he began, addressing us as one beloved person, "a great thing has occurred. My soul has wrestled with the possibility of madness. I teetered between destruction and greatness. But by God, the matter is resolved."

None of us expected this. His distraction had turned to joy. He seemed as exultant as a bridegroom.

"Zaynab, quit looking at your sisters like that. I wasn't mad before, and I am not mad now!"

"Then what are you, sir? Explain it to us simply, so we can understand." Being the eldest—and somewhat spoiled—Zaynab could speak like that, on the verge of insolence.

My father saw that her motive was anxiety. "I want you to celebrate with me, my dear. This is a victory of the soul. I have been touched to the quick by Allah. "

My father caught himself a second time. He could see from our anxious faces that he must compose himself. Once he had, he continued in a calm voice.

"I have enjoyed the fruits of a good life, and another man would have been satisfied. You poor girls have been cursed with a father who cannot close his mind. Ordinary men think it their solemn duty to never open their minds. But I cannot speak for them. All I know is that despite the comforts and love within this house, I have been restless and discontented."

My father spoke without accusation in his voice, but he sensed our disquiet.

"I am not putting even the slightest bit of blame on you. I should ask your forgiveness."

He would have reached out for us, but my mother spoke up. "If you want to calm our fears, do as Zaynab asked. Explain in terms we can understand."

My father bowed his head almost meekly. "I have been leading a secret life. Inside the walls of Mecca, I have played the part of a man who must be like other men. When I walk into the hills, Mecca vanishes like a fever dream. Behind my back those in the clan shake their heads and pity this poor, deluded seeker. They believe in no God and trust none of the gods they do believe in. My secret is that God is not someone you can seek. He is in all things, and always has been. He created this earth and then disappeared into it, like an ocean disappearing into a drop of water. I saw much in my cave, but this mystery was the most important."

Zaynab interrupted him. "Simpler, Papa," she pleaded.

My father sighed. "An angel came to me. He told me that I was God's chosen one."

I will always wonder if Zaynab was ready to shriek or burst into wild laughter. We will never know, because my mother shot her a look like daggers. With all the effort she could summon, her face growing red, Zaynab stayed silent.

"Are angels real?" my mother asked quietly. We all knew, although we never spoke of it, that my father had been talking to wanderers, some of them Jews, others Christians. To an Arab, angels were fantastic, all but unknown.

"Very real," my father said quietly. You could see that he was treading lightly inside, like a man who may be walking on quicksand. "In the middle of the night one came to me in all his radiance. I was wrapped in a blanket on the cold floor of the cave. I shivered when the angel called to me, and at first I didn't know that my trembling was awe, not the cold. I saw a figure arrayed in light standing before me. His voice was commanding, like a soldier who could not be disobeyed, but it was also so gentle that it all but broke my heart. 'Recite!' he ordered."

My father looked around at our little group. We were hanging on every word. "You know, my dear, that he was asking the impossible."

It was true. My father never recites verses or sings songs. It has been a sore point with him since he was a boy with the Bedouin, almost a humiliation. He was only a listener, never a speaker, and listeners win no glory.

"I told the angel I could not recite. You see, even though I was in awe, my mind kept working. I realized that this had to be a dream or a trick of the demons. A notion came into my head that if I talked reasonably to this ghost or *jinn*, a way of escape would show itself. The angel grew in size and brilliance. Twice as forcefully he ordered, 'Recite!' Before I could respond, he threw his arms around my chest and embraced me, to prove that he was no apparition. I cried out, thinking that I would faint—his arms wound around my chest like iron bands. Three times I tried to resist, and three times he seized me in his arms."

You will well believe that my father couldn't remain composed while telling us about the angel. His agitation was strong, and Fatimah began to cry. My mother sent her away with a nurse before Fatimah could plead again, "Where is my papa? I want him back." We heard her wailing die away as the nurse, enfolding Fatimah in her skirts, rushed to the far corner of the house.

"Was that your victory of the soul?" asked Zaynab, who seemed determined to let her doubts speak for her.

"Not yet. I was still too troubled to think," said my father. "When the angel finally released me from his grasp, I dashed out of the cave. My deepest wish was to rid myself of this horrifying burden. To be God's messenger belonged to any other man in the world but me. My heart pounded, and my only thought was to throw myself off the mountain. I beg your forgiveness. In my distraction I failed to think of my family, and the fate that awaited you all if I died. At the summit of Mount Hira I stood on legs as weak as a kitten's, staring down at the rocks below. The angel hadn't followed me out of the cave. That much was a relief. It gave me a few seconds to breathe. Then I looked at the sky, and he was there. The angel towered over me as high as thunderclouds piled up to heaven. I turned around, and he was there behind me, and to every side. I knew at that moment that the form of the angel I saw in the cave was infinitely smaller than his presence. It was an image suited to human sight. The real angel, who came from Allah, lives in Allah. He must be infinite if he is real."

"What do you call this one who came to you?" asked my mother soberly.

"Gabriel. He told me to call him that," my father said.

Now I spoke up. "You haven't told us if you obeyed him. Did you recite?"

My father's eyes gleamed. "That's the miracle, my dear. A humble man whose tongue has no more eloquence than shoe leather suddenly spoke."

My father closed his eyes and held forth:

Recite! In the name of your Lord,
who created human life from congealed drops
  of blood.
Recite, for your Lord is ever bountiful,
he who teaches by the pen,
who taught mankind what was not known before.

As he spoke, my father was transformed. His face glowed; he seemed transported to Paradise. And the verse. I can't explain to strangers how beautifully it fell on the ear, like liquid song. Such precious words couldn't have been his. Where did they come from?

Zaynab broke the spell by suddenly fleeing the room. I looked at my other sister, Umm Kulthum, who had been playing absent-mindedly with her braided hair, the way an infant might pet a doll. "How beautiful," she murmured.

The moment was over. My mother ran down the corridor calling for Zaynab. My father came back to his usual self with a small cough and asked Umm Kulthum if she was all right. A servant ran in to announce that Abu Bakr was at the door.

"Tell him I'm just coming," said my father, adjusting his robe and looking around for his slippers. He wouldn't greet a respected friend in his bare feet.

As he was leaving the room, I grabbed his arm. "Tell me, Papa, what has really happened to you?"

"There is an inner man that nobody sees," he replied. "Now he is on the outside, and the outer man, who is seen by everyone, he is gone forever."

11.

Abu Bakr, Merchant of Mecca

We were only a handful at first. I can't describe how strange we felt, being set apart from society. It wasn't like having the plague. Just the opposite. Imagine that you are starving, driven out of your home to wander the wasteland. In every direction there is only emptiness, and the voice of fear whispers, "Life is nothing but this."

Then one day God spreads a banquet in the desert. Succulent viands, deeply tinted wine, the richest sweetmeats. At first you can't believe your eyes, but soon you have gorged yourself, and lo, a second miracle. No matter how much you eat, the feast renews itself. The table groans with God's bounty.

That was us, starving souls who were fed by Muhammad's words.

"Don't make sheep's eyes at me," he would say. "I am not your shepherd. The only shepherd is Allah. I am just a man among men."

I had known him for thirty years, man and boy, but his humble attitude still amazed me. Wouldn't you want to be worshiped? Anyone who answers no is either lying or has given up on life. Muhammad had done neither. He knew that he didn't cook the feast or make it appear in the desert. He was simply the host who beckoned more guests to come and be filled.

You would have been filled too, sitting at his feet when God delivered a new message. First there was the moment of contact, which was always the same greeting:

In the name of the Lord, who is merciful and compassionate.

We'd never know what would come next. Muhammad himself never knew. God is a master of surprise.

Do you not see how he has lengthened the shadows?
The One is He who made the night a garment for you.
He gave you sleep so that you may rest,
and the morning sky to be a resurrection.

Who had ever seen the night as a garment and the morning as a resurrection? I marveled that God could combine beauty and a promise. It was magical.

I squandered my good name by standing up in the inns, before anyone was drunk yet, and reciting a sura, a passage like that. I felt compelled the way ordinary men are compelled to argue, fight, belch, and make love. With a fresh sura in mind, having run from Muhammad's house, I'd recite things no one could fathom:

He has prepared a bonfire for those who reject the
    hour that is to come.
They will cry out for death,
and He will say, "Do not cry out this day for one
    death, but for many."

Idlers and sots lounging around the wine casks would stare at each other in bewilderment. Why was I ruining their drinking hour with talk of death? Or this:

On the day that the sky is split open and the angels
    stream down in hosts,
true authority will belong to the Lord of Mercy.
On that day the unbelievers will tremble.

Apocalypse is a bad appetizer. But the men couldn't be deaf when it was me, Abu Bakr, who uttered such warnings. I wasn't a crazed half-wit. I had bested most of them in trades and reaped gain from their loss. Muhammad was delighted that I made a spectacle of myself.

"When you stand on a table to speak, they see you standing on a pile of gold," he said. "You're halfway to God already."

Those same men would have scorned my real motive. I wasn't about to gorge myself alone; I had to share the sustenance from heaven. Imagine my sickness of heart when so many people turned away—everyone, if you want the truth. They despised Muhammad's message without even hearing it, like someone who turns his back on a feast because a rumor has spread that the food is poisoned.

It wasn't even a question of believing. Arabs are a murderous race, so our enemies say. If so, we must be murdering in our sleep, because few in Mecca wanted to wake up even when God shook them.

They didn't turn on Muhammad all at once. That's the best I can say. Suspicion spread slowly, like smoke seeping through cracks in a wall. The authorities went on guard first. The Qurayshi elders fixed Muhammad in their steely gaze like hyenas waiting to see if a wounded lion would fight or fall. He didn't do either. One day his gate swung open, and Muhammad walked out, strolling to the marketplace as if nothing had happened.

Muhammad's uncle, old Abu Talib, breathed a sigh of relief. His nephew was respectable again. "If you want the gods to protect you, be harmless," Abu Talib said cynically. "If Muhammad had the slightest power, they would strip it away. At least now he can live as strangely as he wants, so long as he keeps quiet." Abu Talib never lost the bitter taste of his own downfall.

I sat at the foot of the old man's bed and nodded. Abu Talib was right about power. We have a saying: "If power can be bought, sell your mother to get some. You can always buy her back."

Abu Talib was wrong on another point, though. I was sent to tell him the bad news.

"Muhammad will keep quiet in public, but not behind walls. He's the messenger of God. In his mind, everything has changed. He can never go back."

Abu Talib sat up, his face turning red. "In his mind? In my mind I may be the emperor of Abyssinia. So what?" His rheumy eyes narrowed. "What about you? What do you think of this madness?"

"I think we should wait and see," I said.

Abu Talib threw himself back on his pillow. "We're lost!"

The old man loved his nephew. Abu Talib never forgot the promise made to Abdullah's soul, that his son would always find shelter under his roof. Abu Talib knew it would be catastrophic to rock the boat. The Quraysh had nailed down every corner of the city. They had the rats marching in straight lines, people said in private. But Allah can turn a world upside down at His whim. What does Allah care about fat Qurayshi merchants and their padded asses?

I took my leave by telling Abu Talib to get some rest.

He gave another smile, more nervous than cynical this time. "Will you carry a message to the prophet? It's not from God, but it is important. Tell my nephew not to visit my house unless I summon him. I want to die in my sleep." Abu Talib moaned softly, pulling on his wispy beard. "Poor, foolish soul. Tell him I have turned my face to the wall. I don't care if Allah opened his eyes. That's his business. But if he tries to open ours, there will only be trouble."

I brought word back to Muhammad. He took the news calmly. Who was pledged to believe him, anyway? The nearest blood—his wife and daughters; little Zayd, who knew no better, but was devoted to his foster father. And I, who shared no blood with any of them. As long as he held on, Abu Talib was still head of the Hashim clan. Yet with each passing year he continued to spend too many days in bed and lose too much money. He spoke for no one but himself now.

I was surprised how closely Allah watched our movements down here. He had his ear to local gossip, because one day this message came through:

The doubters will say, "How can this be God's messenger?
He walks through the marketplace like any other man."
Tell them, all my messengers have walked through the marketplace like other men.

Before the angel appeared, Muhammad had the town's goodwill. Unfortunately goodwill is like a rose in the desert. Unless you tend it lovingly, it withers overnight. Naturally everyone was glad to see Muhammad back on his feet and among the living. Until he spoke, that is. A man who had cultivated tact suddenly had the unruly tongue of a child. I once took another merchant with me to see Muhammad soon after the great change came upon him. This man was wary, and I wanted the word to go out that Al-Amin was the same trusted man he had always been.

Zayd greeted us at the gate. He was squatting on the ground stringing together a kite. The boy was used to me, but he grew shy seeing a stranger. I complimented him on his kite, which would fly like a bird.

"Not any bird. A falcon," said Zayd gravely. "It will pluck the eyes out of anyone who hurts my father."

The merchant I had brought gave a small, twisted smile, and I hurried him inside. Muhammad was sitting in the back of the house. During that time, I should say, he might get a new message from God at any minute, day or night. No one knew this outside the family. I only risked bringing a stranger, because I knew the signs when Allah spoke to Muhammad. His whole being would change, like a lantern that suddenly has its cover snatched off. If I saw that happening, I could spot a wasp or smell something burning, any pretext to rush the visitor out of the room.

Muhammad beckoned us to sit. We didn't chat, not at first. Whatever you may hear about him from friends or enemies, Muhammad always bore himself with a quiet dignity. This too had been changed by the angel. Now he wasn't simply quiet, he created a silence around him that filled the room like a heavy perfume.

Clumsily, I started up some small talk about business. The visitor felt on safe ground now. He related a tale about a sandstorm that struck his last caravan. It rolled over the camel train like a towering brown wave on the ocean. And when they were no longer blinded, his men found that two camels had wandered away. Even though his men searched for hours, they were never found,

"They swear that the storm blew them into the clouds. And I believe them," said the visitor with a tight laugh. "I had them tortured in a cellar for a few days, and they never broke." He threw his hands in the air. "My loss. You must know how it feels." Muhammad, like any other merchant, had suffered such misfortunes.

Muhammad gave the man a look. I confess, inside I silently pleaded, *Don't talk about God. You need allies.*

In a sober voice Muhammad said, "If you trusted in Allah as you should, He would sustain you in all things. In God there can be no loss."

The man, who was conscious of being the richest person in the room, had never been spoken to in this way. To the most tolerant Quraysh, Allah was the first god among many. To most of them, he was just one more way to squeeze coins out of pilgrims. I could see the man's cheeks start to burn. Before he could respond, Muhammad added, "God sustains us even as

He sustains the birds, which go forth in the morning hungry and return filled in the evening."

The rich man had regained his composure and smiled tolerantly. "Pearls of wisdom," he murmured.

Muhammad's eyes widened innocently. "My words will mean nothing to a glutton, whose bloated belly makes him believe he will never need God."

And that was that. The rich man went pale. "Extraordinary." With one word he sprang up and ran from the room. His hard soles clattering down the hall sounded like a panicked kid goat scrambling to escape from a pack of wild dogs. You will not collapse in shock to hear that he became Muhammad's sworn enemy.

We few who believed in the new prophet began to write down his messages. Each sura came in a distinct way. If Muhammad was about to speak at God's command, his face became shining and full of light. His voice grew higher and more intense. I swear on my soul that one could not mistake this voice for any but the holy Being reaching down from Paradise to this world of clay.

The first time I beheld him in such a trance, my heart was touched. We are not all ignorant in Mecca. On a caravan north to Yathrib, I saw Jews and Christians openly walking the streets and selling in the markets. When I was a child, to see a Jew was the same as seeing a

six-legged calf. I asked someone, who told me that these
were followers of a priest who had come to Arabia on
the orders of God. I asked why. To prepare the way for
a prophet. Then I asked how many believed. The man I
was speaking with opened his arms and said, "As many
as will be received, even some Arabs." So you see, God
was not foolish enough to throw seed on fallow ground.

I asked Muhammad if he heard the words he spoke
when he was transported. "I hear them, and I am as
touched as you. I feel the same awe."

"Then you are a prophet who can share in the joy he
brings," I said enthusiastically.

He gave me a look. It wasn't a chastisement. His eyes
lowered, and he said, "Not the same joy. I must carry
the shame that God speaks through such a cracked
vessel."

The messages grew thicker, and some days they descended like locusts in swarming season. There were
days when you could catch a dozen with one sweep of
your hand in the air. God never spoke unless there was
someone in the room to hear and remember. I sat as
if hypnotized for precious hours. The world has never
been changed from inside a room. I knew that well
enough. But it was hard to show my face without a
mask, until one day I went to the worst side of town
and knocked on a door.

The door was answered by Halimah, Muhammad's old wet nurse. She had moved from the desert a few years earlier. A proud woman in a black shawl mended with a dozen patches. She had outlived most of Muhammad's family with such steel in her spine that she threatened to outlive the rest of us too.

"Come with me," I said.

"I don't see money in your hand. What work do you want me to do?" she replied. Suspicion of the rich was second nature to her.

"The work of a crutch," I said.

Halimah was still quick. She liked riddles. "What kind of crutch does a man need when he has two legs? A loan? I'm not the right one for that. An hour of love to boost his self-esteem? I don't sell my nieces."

I held up my hand. "I need your voice, because mine is too weak." Halimah had heard Muhammad speak and was most moved. Her face lit up almost to match his.

As we walked through the streets Halimah asked no more questions. She followed me to the sacred well in the center of town. As always, women were gathered there filling their water jars and gossiping. They quieted when they saw me. Some stared at my velvet slippers, covered with mud from trudging through Halimah's filthy street, which ran like a sewer.

"Talk to them," I ordered.

Halimah hung back. "What should I say?"

"Repeat what Master Muhammad told us yesterday." I knew she had it memorized.

The old nurse with her missing teeth and lowly station had no reason to believe she had a right to speak. But I've learned that when they repeat a prophet's words, humble people breathe some of his fire. Halimah took all the women in with a slow gaze, and then she recited:

Allah promises a garden to all believers, men and women alike.
Beneath this garden rivers flow, and therein they will abide—
blessed dwellings in Gardens of Eden.
But acceptance from Allah is greater than this. It is the supreme triumph.

I won't say she didn't stumble over a word here and there. Wind whistled through gaps in her teeth. The women at the well were stunned. They stared at each other in amazement. Half of them wouldn't have let Halimah sweep the dust under their feet. Yet no Arab wife or daughter had ever uttered such words. And so many! Halimah didn't know how to react, but she was proud of herself. The angel commanded Muhammad to recite, and now his followers would recite too, over and over.

I ran and told Muhammad what had happened. "Is this how we will change the world?" I asked. "One believer at a time?"

Muhammad replied, "Has there ever been any other way?"

12.

Zayd,
the Adopted Son

I see more than they know. I'm not just a boy to be sent away to fly a kite. I sneak through the shadows and peek through cracks in the door of my father's bedroom. My new father, I mean, the one who gets tears in his eyes when I touch his feet.

I saw him sitting up in bed. His wife—my new mother—was sitting beside him holding out a tumbler. He took a sip. In a low voice she asked, "Do you see him now?"

Father nodded. "He is before my eyes."

Mother looked around. "I see nothing."

"The angel is here. He appeared just as you came in," Father said. "He has come a few times now."

"But he's invisible to everyone else," said Mother, not quite asking a question and not quite making a statement. She was like a bather testing the water to make sure it's not too hot or too cold.

Don't ask me what happened next. I heard little Fatimah running down the hall. She was whimpering, which meant that the next sound out of her mouth would be "Ummi, Ummi," and Mother would come out to answer her. When Fatimah saw me in the shadows leaning against the door, her eyes grew wide. I couldn't be caught there. I said "Ssh" and promised to take her out to play. Fatimah looked at me with a moment's suspicion, but she likes to play better than she likes to tattle.

When I was in bed that night, my mind went back to what Mother was asking. "Do you see him now?" That's what you ask crazy people. *If Father is crazy, then I will be alone again.* That was the first thought that came to me, and I couldn't get it out of my head. Believe me, I tried. I knew I had to be the perfect little boy. That way, even if they drove all the servants away and tied Father to the bed so he couldn't kick and scream the way crazy beggars do in the street, they'd keep me.

This is a house full of chatter and kitchen sounds, clanking pots and maids scolding the nomad who brings milk because it's not fresh. But when my father ran down from the mountain, a strangeness descended over us—the sound of silence. Why is it so frightening? Because it's like the silence before a man is hanged or beheaded. Those things happen to murderers in this city. Murderers and enemies caught on a raid if nobody sends ransom for them. I almost saw a beheading once, before Jafar caught me and dragged me home. Jafar is the cousin I like the best on most days.

The thought that Father had gone crazy was driving *me* crazy. Then I hit on something. What would a perfect boy do? I ran to the cook, who was rolling little balls of dates with honey and almonds. When I asked to help, she looked surprised and said they had girls to do that kind of work. I sat myself next to her and dipped my fingers into the bowl of sticky brown dough. Cook sighed and showed me how to roll the little balls properly, until they were as smooth as marbles.

"Just don't eat any. Master gets them first," she warned. I knew why too. Mother thinks that the candy will sweeten his thoughts. That's another thing I heard. I begged to be allowed to carry the sweets to Father's room. Cook looked over her shoulder.

"You don't want to go in there," she whispered. But I whined, and when she let me trot off with the silver tray covered by a bright red cloth, I think the cook was relieved. At least it wasn't her.

So that's how I got inside Father's room. He looked very tired. His beard was all tangled, and sweat had matted his hair. I tiptoed in and put the tray by his pillow. Then I asked him very low if he wanted some water.

"You can speak up. I'm not dying," he said. "It's not that simple." Who knows what that meant. I fetched the water. He didn't touch it, and he didn't reach for the date sweets. When he caught me staring at the tray, Father pushed it my way.

"Go ahead. It will make them happy to think I've started eating again."

I ate five. You can be a perfect boy and still eat candied dates, right? I'm not sure they made my thoughts sweeter, but I was less afraid. And braver.

"Do you see it now?" I asked.

Father gave me a look. "How do you know about that?"

I shrugged and waited. Either he would jump on me for sneaking around listening at doors or he'd tell me what he saw. I guess he wasn't in a jumping mood, because he sighed and said, "I can't choose to see or not see. He comes when God sends him."

"Sends who?" I asked, with the knowledge that my father always had a special gift.

Pause there. First, I have a riddle. What three-letter word makes a boy invisible if you take it away and makes him visible again if you give it back? I go around asking people this riddle, but nobody ever gets it. When they give up, I walk away.

"Hey, the point of a riddle is that you tell the answer," they all cry after me.

I just smile. "If I tell you the answer, you'll be able to make me invisible." Nobody gets to do that to me again.

The answer is *ibn,* which even strangers know means "son." When you're nobody's son, you're invisible. I never expected it to happen to me. I was tied to my father, Haritha, the way he was tied to his father, as tight as a goat tethered to the back of a wagon. But Allah had other plans and decided to make me as invisible as Himself.

One night I was sleeping under a warm blanket, and then in a moment it was snatched away. A raiding band had invaded our town. Two rough hands bound me hand and foot. They didn't bother with a gag but threw me over the back of a saddle.

This is a dream, I thought.

I heard the horse's hooves clanging over rocks, and its iron shoes threw sparks. The rider who towered over me started to lash his mount to go faster. The tip of his whip caught me in the face. The pain made me wince, and I tasted blood as it rolled down my cheek. This was no dream. The lanterns of the town faded into the night behind us. I had turned invisible.

No one needs to hear the details of what happened next. Allah wanted me to survive, and I did. One day my new father spied me standing in a dirty shift on the slave block in Mecca. I didn't squeeze my eyes shut when they lifted the shift to show that I would be able to breed. Shame doesn't exist when a boy is invisible.

You see why I interrupted my story with a riddle. Muhammad could see me. And if my new father could see me, then I am not surprised that he could see other invisible beings now.

"Who has God sent?" I repeated.

"An angel. Angels are His messengers," Father said.

"And Mother can't see it?"

He shook his head. "She has to ask. And if the angel is there, I tell her where he's standing. She believes me. She says that I have a reputation for telling the truth. Why would I start lying now? Especially with a lie that will make me look crazy."

Now my father's face wore a small, crooked smile. He was making me feel better. Once when I was walking with Jafar, he gave a coin to a beggar who was crouched on all fours, barking like a dog.

"Do you know what makes him a madman?" asked Jafar as we walked away. He was always dropping coins like that, and you never knew who he'd pick to drop one on.

"Because he barks like a dog?" I said.

"No. He's a madman because he doesn't know he's mad."

I kept that in mind, because people do all kinds of crazy things, and it's useful to pick out the ones who have lost their minds. Father was worried that he might be crazy, so that meant he wasn't. I told him so, but he didn't look very comforted.

The worst time for him came soon after that. He kept seeing the angel—he never knew what corner it might be hiding around—but God had nothing to say. There were only two messages. First, when he was afraid and lying in bed, covered with his cloak. God saw Father hiding there, and why not? He can see through walls and hearts and the lies men tell. The angel appeared saying:

> You who are wrapped in your cloak, Arise and
> spread the warning.
> Glorify the Lord's greatness. Purify your garments,
> avoid all that is unclean.
> Do not be weak and overcome. Be steadfast in the
> work of your Lord.

Father immediately told the message to Mother. His heart was torn. Every day made him realize that he was chosen, but who should he warn? Who would listen to him if he did? In her way, Mother had also received a message. Her cousin was old Waraqah, who was blind now and confined to his house. I saw his face only once, and his eyes were clouded over with a white film. Yet the old man's head turned in my direction, even though I hadn't said a word. In secret he became a Christian, Mother said. I don't know that word, but she told me that Christ was as great a prophet as Moses.

"Then why does the tribe hate him?" I asked, meaning the old man, although it was no different with Christ.

As an answer, she quoted a saying: "Blind eyes see more than a blind heart."

I wasn't with her when she ran into Waraqah when he was near the Kaaba. He demanded that his relatives take him there to pray, no matter what threats hung over his head. When he heard that the angel had come to Father, the old man trembled and said, "Khadijah, the holy spirit has come to him. He will be called a liar; they will persecute him. He must hold fast." Mother could see how overjoyed Waraqah was, but she was afraid for him as his voice grew louder. "Holy, holy, holy! He will be the prophet to this nation. But he'll have to fight. If God gives me life, I will be by his side."

Mother tried to calm him. In her heart she was over-joyed and ran home to tell Father everything. Despite this omen the angel brought no more messages. Days passed like weeks. The silence in the house became more anxious.

"If God has something to tell you, why doesn't He do it all at once?" I asked.

"He wants to be sure I'm strong enough. All at once might destroy me," Father replied.

People outside don't know what it did to him to be at God's mercy. We're all at God's mercy. I know that better than most. But for my father it was worse.

I was exhausted being perfect. Nothing I or anyone else did lifted the look on Father's face. Until one day he filled the house with a shout. We all came running. It was a hot morning, and he had woken in a sweat. At that moment a second message had come from the angel. Father recited it quickly, almost out of breath, word for word.

You, wrapped in your cloak. Stay awake through
the night,
leaving half or a little more for sleep.
Recite the Koran, slowly and distinctly.
We are going to send a great message down to you.
When you pray at night, your words will be sharper.

The day's long hours are filled with activity,
so by night devote yourself wholeheartedly to the
  Lord.
He is the Lord of east and west; there is no God but
  Him.

Mother and Father looked relieved. They told me and the girls to sit down to a meal together, like a real family. No one felt crazy that night. Father was smiling the way he did before God arrived. It was like the sun coming out again.

Only to fade in the coming weeks. The great message never came through. We all waited. Father acted the best, even though he had the most reason to be restless and nervous.

"God has told me how to live," he said. "My duty is to obey."

He stayed up half the night praying. My room is close to his, and if I opened my door I could hear him reciting in a strong voice the messages he had already received, over and over. I didn't understand the words, but it brought him peace of mind. This meant we could all stop worrying. I ran out to play again. Mecca is like Paradise to a boy who likes catching rats, chasing dogs, and flying a kite. The months passed, and I almost forgot about the angel. They told me in hushed tones one day that Father had started to receive more messages. He had waited six months. He had started to visit people again, and everyone assumed the crazy times were over. They all breathed easier.

I was pretty sure that it was good for him to hear from God again. In the house Mother said it was good, but I should not talk about it. She saw the worry in my eyes.

"Be happy. God is keeping His promise," she said.

I smiled, acting reassured. On the inside I remembered a saying: "A promise is a cloud. Fulfillment is the rain." I ran outside when I heard my cousins shouting for me. It wasn't raining yet. But I didn't care. When a stranger asks my name, I tell them what Father told me to say: I am Zayd ibn Muhammad.

I'm not invisible anymore.

13.

Ali,
the First Convert

The battle waged against the Prophet is fierce and grows worse every day. It's been seven years now. To protect some of his followers, he sends them across the sea to Abyssinia, where the Christians recognize us as brothers under the same God. A bitter irony, this. Our own blood brothers, the Quraysh, persecute us without mercy. I remain patient, as the Prophet commands. I carry a dagger with me at all times and wait for the day when God will choose the real sons of Abraham.

There's another reason I refuse to run. I lost everything worldly, so that I could gain everything holy. I see that now, as clearly as you see your hand. My poverty doesn't make me ashamed anymore. I used to cringe when thugs laughed at me in the street. My sandals were torn; I barely had a coin to pay a washerwoman to soap the dirt off my robe. When I walk to the Kaaba to pray to Allah, I smile at the wicked. Why shouldn't I? I've secured my place in heaven; no man can strip that from me.

So, you sons of Ishmael, heed the Prophet's warning:

He will not enter hell who has faith equal to a
mustard seed,
and yet he will not enter heaven who has pride equal
to a mustard seed.

I wish I had your courage, to stand at the mouth of hell and not care. You defile the Prophet's name and spit on the ground. That puts him in good company. I've seen men spitting on God in the shadow of the Kaaba. You prideful Quraysh know no shame. You have poisoned Muhammad's camels and spread vicious slanders about his daughters. Your plotting has worked. Didn't Zaynab, his oldest girl, marry a man who refuses to believe? She loves her father, but she fears her husband more.

I've held the hand of a small boy beaten half to death because of a rumor that one of his cousins worships Allah. As his bloody head was being bandaged, I comforted him with Muhammad's promise: "Whoever has seen me, that same man has seen the truth."

So defile me too, that's what I say. It will get me to my reward more quickly.

The faithful tell me that I have the purest blood of anyone who follows the Prophet. My mother was walking past the Kaaba when suddenly she went into labor. To guard her modesty she rushed inside, and so I was born in that holy place. This means nothing to you who pretend that the Kaaba is sacred, but peddle whores within shouting distance of its walls. My mother stayed there for three days until she was well enough to leave. When I opened my eyes, the first face I saw was Muhammad's. He had come to protect my mother the moment he got word of her plight. I was as small and red as a wrinkled crabapple, but he foresaw my destiny. "Name him the exalted one," he said, which is where "Ali" came from.

My father is a sheikh, the same Abu Talib you mock so freely. He was bewildered that I was born in the Kaaba, but he took it as a powerful omen. It wasn't a good omen at first. I nursed at misfortune's breast. I remember being five when the famine struck. Drought wiped out my father's flocks and destroyed the crops in every direction from Mecca. My father couldn't afford to feed me, so one day he sat me on the floor.

"I face shame no matter what happens to you," he said, hardly able to keep from weeping. "The shame of losing you is better than the shame of having you starve under my roof. Seek a better father if you can find one."

I begged to be taken in by my cousin Muhammad. I had known his house since I was old enough to walk. No questions were asked if I grabbed a fistful of dates from the jar and gobbled them down in the corner. When I appeared at his door, Muhammad embraced me and kissed me on the cheek. I became a son to him at that moment, without a word between us. It was like freezing in winter and then suddenly feeling the warm sun on your back.

Let me tell you how the Prophet opened the door of my soul, so that he may open yours. I was eleven when the angel appeared to him. When Muhammad ran down the mountain and hid himself in his room, I was frightened, and what made me most afraid was Khadijah's face the first time she came out of his room.

She took me aside and said gravely, "You must believe. I am not saying this to anyone else. I know you're only a boy, but you must believe anyway."

I asked her why. Khadijah hesitated. "Your cousin Muhammad is now your father. A son's faith begins with his father."

"My father? Abu Talib couldn't even feed me."

Khadijah shook her head. "Abu Talib didn't know it, but he was working the will of God. You were cut adrift to put you under divine protection. Thieves hanging out in the alleys might have stabbed you for a laugh. Instead, you were sent to be the Prophet's son."

She never used the word "prophet" to anyone but me, not in those first days. Muhammad confided to me—this was years later—that he had his own doubts about who he was. He was cowering under the sheets when Khadijah pulled them off and said, "God wouldn't punish a man as righteous as you. I hope with all my heart that you are the prophet promised for so long."

She saw no reason to distrust the angel. So a woman was the first to believe, not me or any other man.

What does a boy of eleven know, anyway? I ran through the streets with my new brother Zayd throwing rocks at stray dogs, peering through cracks in a fence when the camels mated, and wondering why the sight made my body grow hot. By night I asked questions.

"Father, what did the angel look like?"

"At first I imagined that he looked like a man bathed in light. But soon he was transparent and filled the whole sky."

"If I haven't seen an angel, how will I know God?"

"When you know your own self, you will know God."

"But you say Allah is everywhere. If I traveled the whole world, I still wouldn't see Him."

"The Lord has told me, 'My earth and my heaven cannot contain me. The heart of my faithful servant can.'"

And so I believed without question, the way one believes in the sun. Once you set eyes on the sun, how can you doubt it? To sit at Muhammad's feet is like listening to the fountains of Paradise. When new converts present themselves, he puts his hand on my shoulder and says, "Here is my first follower. His face is pure, because it never touched the ground bowing to an idol."

I used to blush to hear that. Behind his back, others argue that I wasn't the first convert, because I worshiped no one before Allah. Therefore, what did I convert from? Nothing. But all of this was secret for the first three years. Muhammad spoke of his revelations only to us few. Then a message came that the entire Hashim clan should be invited to accept the one and only God. I was not yet fifteen, but Muhammad directed me to prepare a sumptuous feast. Forty servings were prepared, enough for every man in the clan.

When the invitation went out, messengers scattered all over Mecca. Muhammad was precise in his instructions. "Don't give the invitation to a servant. Wait at the gate until you get inside or the master of the house comes to you. Bow with respect, and make sure that you use these words: 'Muhammad has spared no expense.'"

The last part was canny. Many people had grown suspicious of Muhammad. They all knew the word "Islam," "acceptance," which he preached. But the Prophet's enemies reminded everyone that the same word meant "submission." "You see? He wants to be chief over the whole city. His God is just a front for his own naked ambition," they sneered. However even the wariest of the Hashim wouldn't miss a great banquet for the world.

The evening arrived; the guests pressed their way though the gate. Muhammad was as good as his word. There was so much food and drink that eighty men could have gorged themselves. The servants were run off their feet; every girl woke up the next morning with bruises from being pinched. I looked around, knowing that every reveler was a doubter. I resented stuffing them with spiced lamb and honey bread, when tomorrow they would only complain about Muhammad louder than ever.

Muhammad was unruffled and reminded me of an old joke to settle my nerves. "A constant complainer died and was sent to hell. When he arrived, he looked around and frowned. 'Is damp wood the best you can burn down here?' he said."

When the company was sated, every man lolling back on his cushion with satisfied groans, Muhammad got to his feet. "Sons of Al-Muttalib, in the name of Allah I know of no other Arab who could have provided a feast like this. I have brought you the best of the hereafter as well as the best of this world. Allah has commanded me to invite you to enter heaven."

Uneasy glances darted around the banquet room. If they hadn't gorged themselves, someone would have grumbled to hear Muhammad invoke Allah's name. A law had been passed forbidding it.

Paying no attention, he raised his voice. "Who will help me in my mission? The one who steps forward will be my brother, my successor, and the leader of the faith after I die."

His call was so passionate that my heart began to race. I gazed around, but the Hashim were looking down at the floor or whispering among themselves. Muhammad asked again for anyone to step forward, and then a third time. I couldn't help myself. I jumped to my feet and said, "I will help you."

Silence.

Muhammad's eyes swept the room, catching a glimpse of every uncle and cousin. None of them moved; a few snickered.

"By the will of Allah," he said soberly, "I declare that Ali is my brother, my successor, and the ruler of the faith after my death. You owe him respect, and you must obey him."

Now the snickering turned to open laughter. One of Muhammad's uncles, Abu Lahab, turned to my father. "See what submission means? From now on, Abu Talib must bow to his son." There was harsher laughter at this, and I could read their angry faces. Every uncle in the room would have to bow to his nephew Muhammad, if they accepted him as God's messenger.

That feast was four years ago, and as events turned out, Abu Lahab became our fiercest enemy. He organized attacks against the believers. He once saw Muhammad praying near the Kaaba and grew so enraged that he grabbed the entrails of a sacrificed goat and threw them all over the Prophet.

Do you really believe he acted out of righteousness? Abu Lahab had already come to Muhammad in secret and asked, "If I accept your faith, what will it profit me?"

"You will be blessed by Allah, as all believers are," replied the Prophet.

Abu Lahab grew impatient. The Hashim had been granted a tithe for the water of Zamzam that the pilgrims drank; everyone accepted this. He asked again what special privilege would come to him if he converted. This time he was twice as haughty.

"To submit is to become humble for God's sake. Your reward will be exaltation in His eyes. What more could you want?" said Muhammad.

Naturally, Abu Lahab wanted much more. He left in a fury and redoubled his denunciations. He wasn't the only rich merchant and trader who feared the call of Islam. To a man they were terrified when their slaves began to follow the Prophet, who went among the poor in secret. In dim houses filled with smoke and the stench of utter want, he raised his hands and said, "Even as the fingers of my hands are equal, so are men equal. None has preference over another." A black slave named Bilal became an eager convert. When his master heard this, he had Bilal dragged by Qurayshi thugs out into the desert, where they beat him and stretched him out in metal armor under the merciless sun.

All the while he murmured, "God is One, God is One." When this was reported to his master, he ordered that Bilal be crushed under the weight of heavy stones. The torture had just begun when Abu Bakr happened to pass by. He ran to the master's house and threw money on the table to buy Bilal. The master hesitated—no doubt to keep teaching his slave a lesson—before he relented. Abu Bakr set Bilal free and began the practice of buying other slaves who had converted.

Panic rose among the Quraysh. After the first three years, the Prophet began to preach in public. The number of believers was still less than forty. But the elders were no fools. They knew the danger of the message and feared a war among brothers. A God who brings all things to those who accept Him is hard to resist for long. Their only recourse was to run to Abu Talib, who as head of the clan extended his protection over Muhammad. Furious as the Quraysh were, they could not break the tribal code. Protection was absolute and had to be honored. If not, there would be endless warfare and blood in the streets.

Abu Talib refused to act. Time and again, his reply to the Qurayshi elders was, "Keep your silence and your dignity. Let us deal with Muhammad the way we must. Our sacred ways are not to be crushed." Abu Talib wouldn't break his promise to take care of his orphaned nephew as his own son.

The Qurayshi elders didn't give up. They found a strapping young man in the slave market and brought him before Abu Talib. "Take this one as your son and renounce the other. The trade can only benefit you," they argued. Abu Talib turned them out of his house with scorn.

I'll tell you what worries the Quraysh the most. It's the mystery of the word. How can this Koran, a stream of words delivered to an ordinary man, be stronger than their swords? Even surrounded by threats and ridicule, people converted, because they heard the voice of God in Muhammad's voice.

If you believe the rumors people spread, Muhammad's followers perform demonic rituals when gathered behind closed doors. If they only knew the truth. Muhammad preaches peace. He says, "The strongest wrestler has no strength compared to the man who can control his anger." Sometimes one of us Muslims—so we call ourselves, to denote that we have surrendered—fights back after being sorely provoked. When brought before the Prophet, he rebukes him gently. "The creation is like God's family. Everything that sustains it comes from Him. Therefore, He loves most whoever shows kindness to His family."

I would never say so in front of the Prophet, but Abu Lahab is the son of the Devil. He watches from behind the scenes like a snake waiting for its prey to come too near. He arranged for the Prophet's house to be vandalized by night. For a time it was necessary to post an armed guard at the gate. Until one day a message came that told Muhammad to send the guard away. God would protect him. Perhaps this sura, one small verse, inspired the Prophet to adopt a new tactic.

He said, "Our father Abraham smashed the idols of his people when they were gone. He mocked these petty gods as lumps of clay that were blind and deaf to the prayers of the idolaters."

After that Muhammad began to ridicule the idols planted all over the Kaaba, inside and out. At dawn he went to greet the new pilgrims who came to Mecca during the holy months, and he challenged idol worship to their faces.

"If your idols, who have no eyes and ears, can protect you from my blasphemy, let them do their worst," he declared. "They won't avail you. In reality they are only the servants of God themselves. Why trust in the slave when you can accept the Master? He alone answers prayers and provides protection."

When the pilgrims saw that none of their gods could harm Muhammad, a few became convinced and were converted. Abu Lahab could not tolerate this, so whenever word came that Muhammad was making his way to the Kaaba, he sent his own men to shout, "Close your ears! A madman is about to harangue you." Their clamor drowned out the Prophet's sermons. After that, he abandoned public preaching and held meetings at night, underground.

Nothing was lost on Abu Lahab, who now had the backing of the entire Quraysh tribe. Instead of crushing the faithful all at once, which even he did not dare, he decided to use a flyswatter. For every new convert to Islam, an old convert would be killed or driven out of Mecca by terror. Muhammad couldn't be touched, not with Abu Talib's protection. But almost everyone else was in danger, especially the servants and slaves who dared to believe differently from their masters.

One day I knocked on the door of an old *hanif* who had come over to our side. The door swung open with a creak. Inside there was no one. I went from room to room, calling out. The old man had vanished overnight, taking his family with him. A demonic symbol had been written in animal blood on the wall.

I ran to Muhammad and cried that the campaign by his enemies was intolerable. "Let me fight back. What else can be done with men who hate you?"

"Do you want to show how much you love your Creator?" he asked quietly.

"With all my heart," I exclaimed.

"Then love your fellow beings first," he said.

After many months neither side could break the stalemate. One man of God with forty followers against every powerful family in the city. Muhammad had no choice but to ask God to bring him a solution.

THREE

Warrior of God

14.

A Jewish Scribe

What strange creatures we are. If you beat a dog, he cringes. If you beat a horse, he runs away. But if you beat a man, he sometimes starts to dream. Such dreams may take him to places you cannot imagine. Being a Jew, I dream all the time.

In my favorite dream, I'm running after bird-catchers. I used to do that for real, long ago. Every spring I'd lie in bed before dawn in my father's house, listening. The bird-catchers never missed a spring. You could hear their captives—finches, larks, and sparrows—singing in wicker cages. Other traders hung bells on their mules, so you would know they were coming from afar. The bird-catchers had no need.

"Did they sell nightingales?" Muhammad asked me one day. It was hot, a few months after he arrived in Yathrib. I was his everyday scribe, and yet there was nothing for me to write down. Nobody was rushing to his house with a divorce for him to judge or a missing bag of wheat that a neighbor had "found" in the street.

"Maybe they sold nightingales," I said. "But they dipped the birds in dye to make them pretty, so you couldn't really tell what they were." A boy couldn't tell, at least.

"Desert birds are gray, but in Paradise they will be brilliant red and green," Muhammad mused. "And their songs will have no longing in them. There is no longing when you are close to God."

"Do birds long for God?" I asked.

"All creatures long for God," Muhammad replied.

He's a dreamer, you see, like me. But his dream holds people's lives together. These Muslims are new to us. They trekked to this faraway city, Yathrib, across the desert two hundred miles from Mecca. Sent by God, they say, as the Jews were sent out of Egypt. The newcomers call it their *hijra,* or "migration." I have no opinion. Maybe their God sent them. Maybe the constant opposition and hatred wore them down.

Here's a joke about being hated. A woman gives birth, and the midwife comes out to greet the father, who is nervously pacing up and down. "Good news," she says. "It's a baby boy, and he's healthy."

But the father still looks worried. "You're sure he's normal?" he asks.

The midwife nods. "He has ten fingers and ten toes. He has a wagging little penis. Oh yes, and he hates the Jews."

The first Muslim I met laughed when I told him that joke. He was a servant to Abu Bakr, who fled here with Muhammad. Affairs had gone from bad to worse in Mecca. Hatred simmered for twelve years after Muhammad met the angel. Abu Bakr built a special structure for prayer outside his house, what they call a mosque. It was obvious no one wanted Muslims defiling the shrines where they kept their idols. This mosque was just four walls open to the sky, where Abu Bakr knelt before God five times a day. That's what Muhammad told them to do. The walls were low, and anyone could look over to see what was happening; the sound of Abu Bakr's devotions filled the street. The elders of the tribe took this as a deliberate provocation.

Muhammad's enemies muttered that no amount of money was enough to keep him from being punished. Muhammad had already proven that the old idols couldn't harm him or his followers. And yet these enemies were right about money not being enough.

Abu Bakr owed his life to a sworn protector who kept the tribe at bay. This protector, Ad-Dughunnah, came one morning and pleaded with Abu Bakr to go inside his house to pray. Instead of relenting, Abu Bakr gave him a hard stare and said, "I release you from your oath. The protection of Allah is all I need."

The hate soon boiled over. The clans of the tribe hatched a plot to get rid of Muhammad without starting warfare in the city. Each clan agreed to pick one strong young man who could wield a knife. As a group, the chosen assassins would set upon Muhammad, each striking him with his dagger. In that way, blame would be equal among all the clans in the tribe of Quraysh. Blood money would be paid to absolve the crime. The new religion would fade away like a parched rose whose water has been stolen. As everyone knew, Muhammad was the water of Islam.

A Muslim merchant was telling me the story, and I stopped him. "Weren't they his own people, the ones who wanted to kill him?"

"He has no people who stand outside God," the man replied.

The appointed night for the assassination arrived. The band of killers stood by the gate of Muhammad's house, holding vigil until he came out for his morning walk at sunrise. They failed to conceal themselves well enough, and inside Muhammad and his devoted young cousin Ali became aware of their presence and the looming danger.

Muhammad and Ali had little time to spare. Muhammad quickly devised an inspired plan. He took a nomad's cloak of green wool that people frequently saw him in. He wrapped Ali in it and told him to lie on his bed disguised as the Prophet.

Ali was reluctant, because he would be leaving Muhammad defenseless. Eventually he was persuaded to obey. Left alone, Muhammad began to recite a verse given to him in a revelation. When he came to the words "I have enshrouded them, so they cannot see," he understood what God wanted. Wrapping himself in a plain cloak, he departed from his house, walking past his assassins without any of them seeing him.

A few streets away he met an acquaintance, who nodded and passed. But the acquaintance was privy to the plot, and he rushed to Muhammad's house and exclaimed that he had just seen him on the street. The band of assassins swore that no one could have gotten past them during the night. To prove it, they sneaked up to the window of Muhammad's bedroom, where he lay asleep, wrapped in his favorite green cloak. The deception was revealed only at dawn when Ali emerged from the house and announced that his cousin had escaped.

Muhammad had made his way to Abu Bakr's. There would be no choice but to flee. Muhammad had received a message warning him of imminent danger. God's will was clear. To stay meant death for all.

With several packed camels, Muhammad and Abu Bakr left Mecca with a small party in haste. They spent three days in a mountain cave outside the city. Ali was left behind to settle Muhammad's business affairs. When he was absolutely convinced that God wanted him to go, Muhammad agreed to cross the desert to his new home in the north.

After I heard this tale, curiosity got the better of me. One afternoon when I saw that he was particularly re- laxed and in good humor, I asked Muhammad, "Do you always trust your messages?"

"It is Allah who trusts me," he said.

"But he sent you into the wilderness. Is that a sign of love? Why didn't he just kill your enemies?"

Muhammad gave me a look. He knows more about the Jews than you can imagine, and the look said, *You're speaking about yourself.* He waited a moment as if deciding what he could tell me.

"I had a wife who believed in me when no one else did," he said gravely. "She heard every word from God and accepted it, to the point that where I ended she began and where she ended I began. Our faith was a second marriage. Her name was Khadijah. One day she was coming to my room with a bowl of soup in her hands. At that moment, just as I heard her footsteps, God spoke to me about her. She came into the room and I said, 'My dear, the Lord tells me that you are blessed. A place awaits you in the Garden, where there is no weariness and only quiet.' She didn't smile, but only gazed at me. We shared the same thought: *this is Allah's way of gently foretelling her death.*"

Sorrow came into Muhammad's eyes. I was touched that he would confide in me, and I had the urge to embrace and comfort him. But the next moment his body stiffened. He said, "Because God tells me the secrets of life and death does not mean that I am the master of life and death. These are great mysteries. By God's mercy I am closer to them than ordinary men. That is just as much a cause for grief as joy."

He never confided in me again, yet I had the strongest feeling that he understood the Jews, because that's how God commands us to live: close to the mystery, but never solving it. Our sorrow and our joy are entwined. Later I heard that Khadijah died soon after that message. It was three years before the Muslims fled Mecca. They call that year Muhammad's year of grief, because his old uncle, Abu Talib, died around the same time. He never converted to Islam, but he blessed Muhammad. They tell me he was hounded on his deathbed by relatives who wanted Abu Talib to give orders against the new faith. He always refused.

One thing I'll grant these Muslims. They pray quietly. They purify themselves and recite the verses taught to them by Muhammad. And they're not lawyers. Before the Muslims arrived, my whole life was lawyers in the rabbis' court. I sat cross-legged in court with my writing table on my lap, scribbling down endless arguments. The judges nodded on the bench, swatting flies that buzzed around plates of sweetmeats. Plaintiffs supplied judges with sweets to keep them in good temper. The lawyers thought they were wiser than the Torah. Them and their niggling minds. One stingy bastard docked me an hour's pay, because he said I smudged a line.

"You smudge the truth, and they pay you more," I pointed out.

He bellowed and kicked me out of court. After that, it was harder to get work with the rabbis, which is why I snatched the job offered by the Muslims. Yathrib has its share of Jews, and too many of us can write.

"You will not take down the Prophet's holy words," they said. "We have our own scribes for that. Your job is to follow legal proceedings, disputes, and daily affairs. When the Prophet renders a judgment, record every word. If he gives advice on any subject,

record every word. This is important. Do you understand?"

I nodded. I wanted the job, didn't I? A few Muslims
had been trickling into Yathrib for several years, but
nobody really noticed them. They made a tiny solemn
group when Muhammad entered the gates at sunset. A
few Jews invited them to take refuge here. In Arabia,
if you worship one God, you want allies. Now that
Muhammad is among them, his people don't just
feel safe; they feel that God has shown them the way.
They've even proclaimed that Yathrib should have a
new name: Medinat al-Nabi, "the city of the Prophet."
If they're in a hurry, they just say Medina.

"Christians also write, perhaps more than the Jews,"
said Muhammad. Because it was hot, I wasn't writing,
as I told you. When I was, he enjoyed watching me, with
a look almost of wonder on his face. For a moment he
wasn't fifty-two with a gray beard, but a child again.

"Christians had to write to survive," I said.

"Why is that?"

"Because the Romans hated their prophet, Jesus,
and they would have killed the lot," I said. "Luckily for
them, the rich Romans were lazy. Many didn't bother
to learn to read and write."

I caught myself, realizing that Muhammad might
take offense. "I don't mean you, sir. You're not lazy.

You work yourself half to death." He smiled, which was rather incredible. Any other rich man in Medina would have given me a swift kick for my insolence.

I went on. "The first Christians were commanded to read their scriptures. They didn't leave it to priests. After a while, so many could read and write that they became useful as scribes. The Romans hired them in the provinces. Time passed, and whenever a new emperor got it into his head to persecute the Christians, his governors would say, 'You can't. Tax collecting will fall apart without our filthy little Christians.' In a few centuries the whole empire became Christian." The irony pleased me.

Muhammad was intrigued. "First they persecute you. Then they need you. In the end, they convert to your religion."

He repeated this to himself several times that day. Later on, I figured out why. No one in power needs the Muslims, not yet. There are not many of them, not enough to form a decent armed tribe. He's worried about how they'll survive. God commanded him to spread the good news, like Jesus, but how?

The Muslims told me that in Mecca Muhammad would sit near the town well every morning teaching his followers. If a servant came by, he could sit and listen along with everyone else. Even a slave could sit and learn.

The high-born people didn't like this, but they wouldn't draw near, because you don't talk to a respectable man with slaves hanging about. Finally one of the elders came to Muhammad, saying, "I wish to have words with you, brother. Send the slaves away."

Muhammad nodded as if he consented, but suddenly he couldn't speak, and his face broke out in a sweat. Receiving no answer, the elder stormed off. A little after that, a new message came to Muhammad: "Do not drive the believers away or you will be among the evildoers." So he had no choice. He had to save every idol worshiper in Mecca, rich or poor. The task seemed impossible. When Muhammad went to the fat elders of his tribe, they ridiculed the notion that one of their own was chosen by God. When he went among the poor, they were too easy to convince. They would hope for favors and money from a wealthy merchant who suddenly paid attention to them.

"Did he find an answer?" I asked one of the Muslims.

The man shrugged. "Would we be here if he had?"

I meet Jews who are suspicious of the newcomers. I tell them that Muhammad is like Moses leading his lost children, but they mock, "And Yathrib is their promised land? Where's the milk and honey? They should keep moving."

I went to Muhammad and asked him if this was their promised land.

"That's not my concern," he replied. "God can find his own anywhere on earth. There's something more important." He pointed to a pile of scrolls on the floor. "This is God's book. It has been growing for twelve years now. Nothing is more precious. You are people of the Book, so you understand."

I drew back. If I said yes, I understand, would that make me a bad Jew? Is it a sin for me to work for a Muslim whose book isn't mine? I hear the whispering in my mind, and to the people of the Torah this is what I say. If the messiah comes tomorrow and drives the Gentiles into the sea, maybe he will turn to me and say, "Eli, dear boy, sit at my right hand. I will be busy rebuilding the Temple of David. You take care of business while I'm away." Then I would rule the world and nobody's God would be before mine.

But there is no messiah, no Temple, no way around the Gentiles. I must wander like Joseph among the unbelievers, only I don't weep. I adapt. And if these Muslims have found their own Elijah or even Moses, why should I kick the cow that gives me milk? My job is to write, not to judge. I've never seen Muhammad when he gets his messages, which keep coming, they say. New scrolls appear around him. Some days I'm not allowed in the door. Other days I see him begin to change. His eyes roll upward; he trembles slightly, like a sparrow you hold in your hand. At the first sign I'm driven out of the room.

One thing I do know. Muhammad hands down their laws, just like a Moses. So if a prophet says, "God told me this," and his followers say, "We believe you," how can anyone disprove it? When I am safely behind my own door I can light candles remembering the Maccabees, who died as heroes defending the Jews, and I can curse our enemies. There's time enough for that. Always time enough for that.

Muhammad hasn't passed fifty without gaining some canniness, and he saw these warring thoughts in my mind. One day he told me to put down my writing tablet. "Look in my eyes," he said. "Do you see a fraud and a liar?"

I was too startled to reply.

"If you don't see a fraud and a liar," he said, "then I am telling the truth. God has made me His messenger."

I was embarrassed and mumbled something, I can't remember what.

Muhammad became stern. "Don't risk your soul. God commands me to save the Jews. He wants me to save the world."

Muhammad paused, and for a moment I was afraid he wanted me to make a choice, then and there. But he looked away instead and continued.

"For three years I couldn't even tell my uncles and cousins. Do you know what anxiety I felt? To know from God's mouth that all sinners are damned. He sees everything. He marks every deed we do on earth, and at the last day the damned will testify against themselves out of their own mouths. Can that day be far off?"

My heart was pounding. There was steel in his voice as he spoke, but not the steel of a madman. Muhammad got his strength from something outside his body. A force like lightning that can turn a soul to ashes or forge it in flames.

I stammered, "Don't ask me to believe. But I can see. You survived the fire."

He looked surprised. "Do you see that? Because it's true."

I lie awake wondering if the world will come to an end before the next sunrise. My mind still goes back to my childhood when I waited for the bird-catchers. Sometimes a bird would die suddenly. Maybe they gave it the wrong food, or maybe it had a broken heart from being separated from its mate. The bird-man would pluck the feathers of a dead bird and weave a fantastic cap for himself, glittering with every hue, more than a rainbow. You could hardly tell the catcher from the catch.

I hope Muhammad gets to see the birds in Paradise, as God has promised. And I hope I'm not left out when that day comes.

15.
Fatimah, Muhammad's Youngest Daughter

The faithful are readying for war. The night I found out, I had a nightmare. A pack of hyenas brought down a lion, and they started to gnaw at its carcass while it was still alive. The hyenas laughed as they pulled out the victim's entrails; the lion roared with defiance as it died. I woke up trembling and uttered one word: *Father.*

I must have shouted without knowing, because Ali, sleeping beside me, rolled over and mumbled. I held very still until he fell asleep again.

Is this coming war a test from God?

The summer caravans leaving Mecca all travel by Medina on their way to Syria. They are Qurayshi caravans, most of them, and the grandest have a thousand camels. From a height it must look like a trail of ants creeping from horizon to horizon. Most of our Muslims are poor. A few farm on the tiny plots of land they are begrudged. Many others try to trade, but struggle in a foreign city where no tribe is their own.

Hauling a small cart of crops to market with limited prospects for the week, a hungry Muslim is passed on the road by camels loaded with silk, jewels, and spices. The temptation to raid is great.

When the raids first began, they were no different from the custom of poor Arabs trimming some extra fat from the rich. The caravans were disrupted for an hour and moved on. Ali was amused. "Half the time they can't find the caravans and come home empty-handed. The desert needs to be smaller."

It was sport, a game. The nomads have been playing it since the time of our ancestors. If captives are taken, they can be ransomed. In the meantime, captives and captors sit around the same campfire and sing songs. One never hears of killings, because then a blood feud would erupt, and that means trouble on both sides.

Now everything has changed. It started when one of our real fighters, Abdullah ibn Jahsh, went south on the trail close to Mecca, risking greater danger. His raiding party found a small caravan camped in a palm grove. Three timid merchants guarded a few scrawny camels. When Abdullah's band descended on them, the first arrow from Abdullah's bow pierced a merchant in the heart. The shot was intentional. Shocked, the other two fell to the ground in surrender. They were marched to Medina, and Ali's amusement changed. The mob didn't greet Abdullah as a hero, but as a violator of the peace.

"Look at the rabble." Ali pointed out the window at the grumbling people in the street, Jews and Arabs who had once welcomed us. They were disturbed and angry. Sport had gone too far. Rumors spread like wildfire that Abdullah had defiled the holy month of Rajab, when no fighting is permitted. His attack was unholy, and many thought that he had the blessing of Muhammad to commit violence. Confidence in the Prophet was badly shaken.

"It's not our holy month," Ali argued. "It belongs to the idol worshipers. How can we be bound by our enemy's customs?" Ali fumed when word came that a few poets in the marketplace were making up songs ridiculing the Prophet.

We had been married only a year. The whole time I hid my face from the raids and never asked if Ali was part of them. Then he brought me the news. A message had come to Father from Allah: "It is permitted to fight." The message was longer than that. It spoke of those who had unjustly been persecuted for worshiping one God and driven from their birthplace.

God was favorable to Abdullah's raid. A lesser crime by a Muslim was forgiven when the weak were oppressed, because that is a greater crime before God. But all I heard was the phrase that changed our lives. *It is permitted to fight.* Ali's excitement matched my fear.

"Faith, purity, blessings," he said. "They aren't enough to defeat evil. Sometimes it takes blood."

He squeezed my hand in reassurance, but it wasn't his words that frightened me. It was the look in his eyes. I couldn't bear to look back. A battle. Whenever it came, he would rush to fight on the front line. A defender of the faith could do no less. I've never seen a battle, but you don't have to see one to know who dies first. I took my hand away, so he couldn't feel my fear.

"Aren't we here to bring peace?" I asked.

"If we are wiped out, there will never be peace. This isn't an evil choice, because it's no choice at all. The enemy has decided to come for us."

When I was a girl, a runner pounded on the gate demanding to see Father. His face was bloody, and he was filthy from running all the way to Mecca from the hills. A small party of the faithful had sought a remote place to worship in peace, but the Quraysh had them followed. In the middle of their prayers they were set upon by attackers with knives and clubs. My father blanched and listened gravely to the runner's account. The faithful were strong young men; they drew as much blood as they lost. It wasn't enough for the Quraysh to forbid trade with anyone who dared to follow the Prophet. They resorted to torture, especially if one of the faithful was a slave. An adopted son of my mother's was stabbed in the Kaaba itself.

Ali's eyes reminded me of all this. I prayed for God to give me words. "At least you won't have to buy your shield back," I said.

His face flushed scarlet. It was cruel to bring back bad memories. I felt ashamed. But how much crueler for warriors to butcher each other.

Here is how Ali lost his shield. When we came to Medina last year, Father had begun to unite the people. He brought peace between the Jewish tribes and the Arab tribes, who had been fighting for three generations. For the Jews it was an eye for an eye; for the Arabs it was blood feud. Both sides could never forgive any harm done to their clans. But a hundred years of violence had exhausted them. They turned to Father, who brought his reputation for fairness with him to our new home. A peace pact was drawn up, and both sides placed their hands on one another, swearing to keep the city safe and to protect the poor.

When everyone was gone Father shook his head. "Oaths aren't enough. Pacts and treaties aren't enough." There had to be other ways to bond the tribes of Medina, because he knew that the Quraysh would come one day. He chose a partner for each Muslim man among the Arabs of the city, forming a brotherhood. Yet he knew the strongest bond was blood, and blood means marriage. I was innocent of all this. A seventeen-year-old thinks of a husband, I know, but Father was in grief over losing Mother. I sat at his feet every day, and even though he would marry again, he would never love anyone as he had loved her. Between us it was understood.

How amazing one day when I entered his room and Abu Bakr smiled at me. He always smiled to see me, but a woman knows the difference. He wasn't smiling like an uncle. There were only a few men who lingered at our house, men trusted by Father to tell him the truth at all times. Umar, who is very wise, also began to smile at me, and Ali, the cousin who had been part of our household as long as I can remember.

"A smile was all I had," Ali would recall with a grimace.

It was true that he was poor. When they heard that Father needed a son-in-law to strengthen the faith, Abu Bakr and Umar offered themselves in open proposals. Father held up his hand. Everyone waited. Time went by, and still no decision. Ali could hardly stand it. I wasn't a child anymore asking him to look for my doll, and he had sat in council with men for eight years. Without money he couldn't even make a bridal gift. One day he came into Father's presence and sighed.

"What is it?" Father asked.

Ali was startled. "I said nothing, sir."

"Ah, I thought you were asking for Fatimah."

Father loved Ali dearly, and he gently suggested that Ali owned one thing of value, a shield chased with silver edges. He could sell that to get money for the bridal gift. Ali took heart and obeyed. Then Father came to me and announced that it was God's will for me to marry Ali. Would I consent?

Something tied my tongue. Fear of leaving my beloved Father? Ignorance of what passes between a husband and wife? Ali had hidden his desire so completely, out of respect for Father, that he hadn't even made sheep's eyes at me. Before I could find anything to say, Father smiled. "God has made you silent. I know in your heart that you agree." I realized he was right.

We were married here in Medina a year after Hijra. The Muslims, surrounded by strangers, were grateful for something to celebrate. My sister Ruqayah gathered all the women to cook the feast. The carpeted floor was crowded with dates, figs, lamb, and wine jars. It was like being home again. As many tears were shed for that reason as for joy. The whole company laughed when the richest guest, Uthman, who had married Ruqayah, rose to present a gift to the groom. With a flourish he brought forth Ali's shield. Uthman had paid for it, but refused to keep it. Father's eyes twinkled. There are ways to sell things and still not lose them.

It displeased my husband to be reminded by me now that he couldn't buy his shield back himself. I sighed. The same shield would protect him when the battle arrived. What strange paths Allah takes to work His will.

"I can't stop you," I said. "If you are a *ghazi*, God be with you."

"What is a *ghazi* to you?" Ali asked. How could I find the words to reply without offending him? Already I felt the heat from his burning cheeks.

"A *ghazi* is someone who strives for the sake of God," I said.

"And is there a limit to striving?"

I cast my eyes down. "No, dear husband."

"Well, then. Peace be upon you."

"And you."

Ali seemed satisfied. A stranger would be baffled by this conversation, I know, and all that it meant for the future. Perhaps our whole destiny depended on a shifty word. *Ghazi* means striver, but it's also what we call the raiders. It was an innocent term before Abdullah's arrow drenched it in blood. Now no one strives for Allah in peace. The *ghazi* provoke fights with the Quraysh. They declare that Allah ordains them, and suddenly their raids are holy. The logic of men is hard to unravel from the logic of God. He must see a purpose to all this violence.

Troubled, I ran to Father when he was alone. He sits in the dark brooding when he isn't in council. Medina has made him turn gray—but fierce too. His manner is so stern that some of the faithful fear him as much as they fear Allah.

"Why does God want blood?" I blurted out.

"A bold question from such a timid child," he muttered. It was the closest to a rebuke I had ever heard from his lips. But I'd rather be loved for truth than meekness. I asked him again.

"God doesn't want blood," he said. "He wants warriors when the unjust persecute the just. The faithful are made strong by defending their faith. Otherwise they will scatter like leaves when the next storm comes."

"But the *ghazi* provoke the enemy."

"They strike before being struck. God forgives them. He knows that the enemy has done violence to us for fourteen years already. He wants the balance redressed."

These were hard words to hear from Father. It was as if he were speaking in the mosque. But when I gazed into his eyes, they weren't fierce; they were pleading. He went to the window and closed the last open shutter, making it night in the room.

"Don't try to read my mind, child. It isn't mine anymore. God commands everything, even my thoughts. I must obey."

I ran away to console myself. How easy for his enemies to say that Father is hiding behind God. How convenient that these raids that infuriate the Quraysh have a divine blessing. I had to know the truth. It was shameful for a daughter not to believe her father. I do still believe him. Yet in my mind's eye I saw Ali's corpse being dragged across the battlefield, leaving a track of blood in the sand. I had to know.

I broke into Abu Bakr's room in distress. He was doing something he didn't want me to see and barely had time to hide it.

"A sword?"

He sheepishly brought it out from behind his back. "This old arm can barely swing one. I practice every day."

Abu Bakr is a second father to me. He read my heart. "The Prophet isn't here to bring messages. He is here to bring justice. Look around you. The tribes of the city keep the peace. We have laws and safe places to worship. God protects the sons of Abraham as long as they obey him and bring his words to pass."

I felt a spark of hope. "Then He won't allow any Muslims to be killed?"

Abu Bakr gave me a wry smile. "Certainly not a man as strong and brave as Ali."

I blushed. "I wasn't asking just for myself."

"Then hear me. If we fight for justice, it isn't violence. It's a righteous act. When righteousness remains passive, the unjust show no mercy. The nature of evil is to spread, like a contagion."

This was a long speech for him, but not a practiced one. I know Abu Bakr. He risked everything in Mecca to stand beside Father. He broke blood ties and walked among assassins with his head held high. If anyone knows what a righteous act is, he does.

Abu Bakr hesitated. "I don't think you realize. The Prophet led one of the first raids. He became a *ghazi* when God commanded him."

I was shocked, and yet I wanted the truth. Abu Bakr assured me that none of the early raids drew blood, or were meant to. Father had ridden out, because one of the greatest enemies of the faith owned the caravan. Like the others, this raid came to nothing, because the scouts couldn't locate the camel train in the vast reaches of the desert.

If that made me grateful, it was only for a moment. Allah began to weave a mystery around us, and like men stumbling in the dark the Muslims wandered into a scene whose outcome was known only to Him. It began when news came that the richest caravan of the year was heading home to Mecca. Its leader, Abu Sufyan, hated the Prophet. He accused him of wanting to destroy the tribal order, but we all knew Abu Sufyan's secret grievance. When a small group of frightened Muslims had fled across the sea to seek refuge in Abyssinia, his own daughter was among them. The Quraysh sent an ambassador to convince the Negus, king of Abyssinia, to send the refugees back to Mecca. Lavish bribes were laid at his feet, and evil might have won the day. That is, if not for a leader of the refugees who read verses of the Koran to the Negus, who as it turned out was a Christian. Hearing the word of God and knowing how dearly we Muslims held the prophet Jesus, the king sent the ambassador home in scorn.

Abu Sufyan never forgot his loss, for which he held Father to blame. His persecution was ruthless. "But now he's coming within our grasp," Ali said. He pressed Father to attack the caravan. At one stroke he would have revenge on his enemy Abu Sufyan and seize wealth for the suffering Muslims. On its long trek, the caravan had to stop at the Well of Badr for water. It was a perfect place to lie in wait.

Suddenly the streets were full of noise, as if the men were preparing for a festival. I hid inside, praying that Father wouldn't concede to this bloody adventure. It wasn't his decision alone. He wasn't the military chief; he had to seek counsel from all the leading men. The air was filled with piercing calls to war. Volunteers ran to the central square. Delirious with dreams of plunder, seventy Muslims who had come from Mecca volunteered. To everyone's astonishment, more than two hundred more from among the converts in Medina volunteered.

Ali ran in with an exultant look. "Soldiers have sprouted like wheat sown with God's hands." For the first time, the faithful had more than devotion on their side. They had numbers.

Foolish dreamers. They marched out of Medina like nomad boys pretending to be the Roman army (not that any had ever seen Romans, who could be invisible gods for all we knew). Women stood at the gates singing Bedouin war cries to make their men strong in battle. I lay in my darkened room with a pillow pressed to my face, but I heard their shrieks, which were like wild animals.

How foolish we are here believing we act for ourselves, when God is the only mover. He began to play cat and mouse, not telling either side which one was the cat.

Abu Sufyan had good spies, and one of them, seeing the march out of Medina, ran up the trail to warn him of the ambush at Badr. Abu Sufyan was crafty and intelligent. He immediately turned his caravan off the trail toward the sea, hoping to march around Badr and get his water by trade with the nomads who control the coastal roads. At the same time he sent a runner to Mecca.

This runner caused panic when he arrived. He tore is shirt and screamed hysterically. "Merchants of Mecca, heed me! Your goods are never coming back to you. Muhammad is stealing your money and your camels. Heed me or be lost!"

A girl must never show how much she knows about boys, or women about men. But we all knew that Meccans weren't fighters, except in show. Battle was a dance where the negotiations for peace came before any fighting broke out. Craftiness brought more victories than a sword. Yet this naked threat to their wealth enraged the Quraysh, and one of father's chief tormentors, Abu Jahl, blocked any talk of a treaty. He quickly assembled a thousand soldiers to march to Badr. "How many men can Muhammad have?" Abu Jahl argued. "Fifty? A hundred?" Suddenly fired with courage, the Qurayshi army left Mecca with the same festive air and passing of the wineskin as our men left Medina. God made both sides believe they were the cat.

When Father and our men arrived at the Well of Badr, no one was there. They waited anxiously, and eventually two water carriers appeared to fill their jugs. They were captured and bound, then led before Father after a sound beating had loosened their tongues.

"Where is the caravan you bring water to?" he demanded.

The two water carriers were bewildered. "Caravan? We come ahead of the army of Abu Jahl, which is a few days away."

At this the Muslims almost lost heart. They realized that there would be no plunder, and worse, instead of overcoming thirty or forty guards who traveled with Sufyan's caravan, a bloody-minded army was coming for them. For the first time, the wiser heads suspected that God was weaving a mystery. Or was it a trap? Abu Bakr rose and argued that God wanted a battle to settle the Qurayshi threat.

"They threw us out of the tribe. They branded us as a band of traitors," Abu Bakr pointed to Father, who sat silently as his chiefs held council. "Our very Prophet they ridicule and mock. God cannot abide these evils. We must stand and fight."

Abu Bakr's speech rallied the seventy Muslims from Mecca. To everyone's astonishment, the new converts pledged to fight without surrender. Only a few voted to return home to Medina, citing as their goal plunder from a caravan, not war.

Father thanked his men and retreated into his tent. Up to that moment, God had never asked him to lead an army. He felt the dreadful guilt of someone responsible for the lives of many. At the same time, he trusted that God would lead his steps and guide his hand.

When Abu Jahl came over the last dune to confront the oasis at Badr, he couldn't see the Muslim forces. They had camped out of sight, and many of the Quraysh were relieved. They had gotten news that their goods were safe; the caravan was out of Muhammad's grasp. As true devotees of money, they saw no reason to fight once their god was safe. A band turned back to Mecca, including some of the Hashim and others who were anxious at the prospect of fighting their own relatives and friends. A new faith doesn't turn a cousin into a stranger.

God's game went deeper than blood ties. Abu Jahl had wild ambitions. He was already powerful, but by saving the caravan of his rival, Abu Sufyan, he had pulled off a coup. Soon word would be spread by every wandering poet in Arabia that Sufyan was the protector of the Quraysh, beloved by the gods. The only move that would surpass this was for Abu Jahl to defeat the Muslims and bring the Prophet to his knees. He argued for war, and with reluctant muttering the clan chiefs agreed to stay.

They drank wine in their tents to calm their nerves while a scout named Umayr climbed the dune that looked down on the Muslim camp. Umayr returned with a pale face and wild look in his eyes. Instead of seventy or a hundred men, Muhammad had gathered three times that many. The Meccans started muttering anxiously. Abu Jahl remained stubborn, however, pointing out that the Qurayshi army was more than twice that size, almost three times, even after the recent defections.

"I've seen the faces of these Muslims," Umayr replied. "They are set for death. You will not kill one of them before they have killed one of you."

Abu Jahl publicly scorned this prediction. In his heart of hearts he realized that the old Bedouin game of ritual fighting and bickering was over. This new enemy would fight and never negotiate. There was another thing that only he and his chiefs understood. My father had taken the valley and surrounded the wells. Without water, the Quraysh had no choice but to fight, even though they were forced to climb uphill facing the sun to get in place. How could the gods have done this to them?

They had one hope to avoid massive bloodshed. All Arab battles began with single combat. Three men from each side, chosen from the cream of the armies, came out to fight hand to hand before the main forces charged. Often this was enough to end the strife, and if not, Abu Jahl trusted that his three champions would slay the other three and fill the enemy with fear.

I know you wonder how a woman can speak of these matters, so I must tell you that my worst fear came true. Ali was among the three chosen to fight hand to hand. He strode out into the morning sun with his sword and the very shield that had brought his love to my bed. As soon as the call to fight sounded, he rushed forward and within seconds had stuck his blade through the body of Walid ibn Utba.

I wept as he told me all that I have told you. "God held my hand, and He struck the blow," Ali said. The man he had slain was an avowed enemy of the faith and the son of Utba, whose hatred was even greater.

Can a single thrust decide an entire battle? Perhaps this one did, for all three Qurayshi champions were killed and only one Muslim, who sustained a wound that proved mortal. The two armies had to engage. Abu Jahl knew that he still had more than two fighters for every Muslim. But a powerful transformation had overcome my father. In the night God taught him how to be a warrior. It was revealed that the Muslims should form a tight band, raining arrows on the Quraysh as they stumbled down the hill, blinded and confused by the sun in their eyes. Only at the last second, when the enemy was close, should the Muslims drop their bows and charge with drawn swords.

Abu Jahl had no notion of such warfare. He had fought in desert skirmishes before. Even in the fiercest ones each fighter was on his own, and there were no tactics, just a melee as disorganized as boys having a mud fight. His men fell back under a hail of arrows. They tried to stagger forward, and another hail of arrows hit them. Still packed together, the Muslims charged. In panic the Quraysh dropped their arms and ran. The whole battle was over before the afternoon sun was halfway down the sky. When the enemy dead were counted, many were leading chieftains, and one was Abu Jahl himself.

Immediately the victors began to round up the wounded to slaughter them, but God sent Father a message that none were to be killed. It was enough to march them back to Medina and hold them for ransom. He stopped the wild looting of the enemy camels and weapons, decreeing that the spoils should be shared equally among all the clans who had fought so courageously.

"It was a day of joy," I said quietly. At least my Ali had survived, which was joy enough. Until the next time.

He understood why I was solemn. "Dear wife, your father was not exulting. He knew that the Quraysh have reason for more revenge now and more attacks. No one could mistake the tears on his cheeks for tears of joy."

The Prophet had foreseen the repercussions. Allah had tested him with anxiety, doubt, and bloodshed. Only then had He revealed who was cat and who was mouse. God, the all-powerful and all-knowing, planned every move on both sides. He alone knew what was needed for the faithful to win. Therefore, nothing less than total obedience to His will was acceptable. Without that, the enemy would never relent. This victory at Badr would be the end of the Muslims unless Father heeded every revelation to the letter.

"Have you heard about the angels?" Ali asked. In the ecstasy of winning, soldiers had spread the word that a host of angels had appeared overhead as they fought, indicating that Allah was on their side. When Father heard that Gabriel himself had joined them, he nodded and smiled.

"Do you believe that?" I asked Ali. I had no idea what his reply would be. I knew what the old Ali would have said before he marched off. He would have revealed his doubts. A new Ali returned, though, and something about him made him seem like a stranger.

"Angels are good for the troops," he replied. "None of them ran, even when we were outnumbered. Only God can inspire a man to fight under those conditions. Allah has revealed how we'll survive."

My heart sank. "Through war?"

Ali shook his head. "Not just war. Holy war."

He was using a peculiar word new to my ears. *Jihad.*

16.

Ibn Ubayy,
the Hypocrite

I walk through Medina, and the same thought torments me. I was born to rule here. No more. It's all Muhammad now. I smile, and on every side they smile back. I am given respect, just as before. No one can see how my mind grinds and grinds.

Beside me is one of the last chiefs of the Khazraj tribe I can trust. I tell him, "The Prophet has created a paradise. Use your imagination. It's all around us."

He isn't immune to irony. "Soon the camels will be dropping manna. Be careful not to step in it."

How long did it take for me to lose everything? Four short years. The Muslims were hanging on by a thread back then. I was on the rise, because the warring tribes in the city looked to me to bring peace. The Jews were ready to forge an alliance with the Arabs. If I could stop the endless blood feuds, I would be the chief of chiefs. Some even whispered a daring word: Ubayy the king.

"The mosque," my companion says, warily pointing up ahead. We are going to pray, the two of us. It's not safe to speak ill of the Prophet this close to the mosque.

I hear you laughing. Ibn Ubayy a Muslim? You don't understand. Conversion is about power. The God of Muhammad has cast down the gods of Arabia. They have crumbled to dust.

I remember the day the warriors came home from Badr, two years ago. We were waiting along the city walls, ready to behold a broken column bringing the dead and wounded. We couldn't believe our eyes when we saw the corpse of Abu Jahl instead, dragged on a bloody litter behind a mule. The wind turned that day. I felt a shudder run through me. If their God could crush the Meccans with a handful of soldiers, anything was possible. Six months later, my forehead was touching the ground in the mosque.

As we near the door to pray, my companion looks around nervously. We're lucky this morning. No one assaults us or spits on our feet. A few mutter an oath. *Munafiq*—"hypocrite." When I overhear them, I lower my head humbly. Isn't that what God commands the faithful to do, submit?

Kneeling in the cool dim space where the Prophet's word is law, I feel lonely. I once wore my people like a cloak, wrapped tightly around me. I rose step by step, keeping careful watch. Ambition isn't a banner you fly overhead as you march down the street. It's a ladder just tall enough to steal all the fruit from the tree. Preferably at night. Muhammad understands this, and so do I.

Hundreds of men surround me at prayer. As we murmur to Allah, a ripple runs through the crowd. Eyes cautiously peer to the right and left. The Prophet himself has entered. No one has to say so. His presence is enough.

I'm bold and lift my head as he passes. Age has not bent him, nor care made him weary. Why should they? He's the victor. His robe is gleaming white; he bestows a blessing with a wave of the hand. Half a dozen bodyguards form a shield around him, but through the cracks Muhammad spies me and frowns slightly. I'm not the only hypocrite in this paradise. We form a party, in fact. Arabs who jumped to the new religion because there was no other choice. I couldn't change my ways to suit the Prophet. He calls me a thorn in his side.

Once when I challenged him, he became too angry to speak.

"Don't turn your face from me," I said. "Embrace me. I'm the one you must save."

"First you must want to be saved," he replied. "Your eyes must open to God."

"Is that why so many lying in the street have their eyes closed?" I shot back. "Or is it because they're dead?"

I went away holding back my anger, but my tongue betrayed me. I was overheard telling one of my cousins, "This is what comes of bringing strangers among us."

So far no message from God has come to make me disappear, not the way so many others have disappeared. I mean the Jews. We had three tribes of Jews in Medina when Muhammad arrived. If they hadn't planted the seed of one God, Muhammad would never have come here. The Jews made a garden in the desert for him. One day I was their champion, the judge who would bring peace to all the tribes. I woke up the next day, and their doors were shut against me. Muhammad would be their judge. Muhammad was the bringer of peace.

Then the tide turned against the Jews. The people tell a tale that could be true. One day a Muslim woman had come to market in the Jewish quarter. Sellers at their stalls called out, "Let's see your face. What's wrong, are you too ugly to behold?" They were used to ogling. Muslim women wear a veil.

On this day a goldsmith grabbed the woman and pinned back her clothes so that her face was revealed; he threw her to the ground, and when she arose, her clothes were snatched off, leaving her naked. A Muslim man heard the commotion, ran to the scene, and killed the goldsmith with his knife. In turn, the Jewish sellers killed him. A blood feud was ignited.

Muhammad laid siege to the Jewish quarter. And after fifteen days the dominant tribe, the Qaynuqa, surrendered. Having seen that seven hundred armed Jews could be summoned to fight against him, the Prophet felt the danger in his midst. He banished the Qaynuqa from Medina. How do the Jews feel now scraping for a living in the barren countryside and distant villages?

I went before him and pleaded their case. "We had fierce battles before you came to Medina," I declared. "In one battle the leaders of both sides were slaughtered, and I was saved only because the Jews of the Qaynuqa defended me. They are strong. They will help defend you when the Meccan army marches on the city."

Muhammad had just returned from Badr, and my timing was wrong. He was swollen with the arrogance of victory. Why did he need Jewish warriors? They were the real thorn in his side, not me. Their quarter of

Medina became a ripe plum for the Prophet to pluck. He confiscated their property and divided it among the faithful.

From that day onward, I earned the name "hypocrite." What name should I lay at the feet of the Prophet? In time the second tribe of Jews was banished. Those of the third tribe were called traitors for siding with the Arabs of Mecca. Was it true? They were traders. Their fortunes depended on going to Mecca, where the great market thrives. Perhaps the Jews only wanted for life to go on as it had in their fathers' and grandfathers' time. Perhaps they were unlucky, plotted against the Muslims, and lost. Suddenly there were beheadings in the street. Traitors were to die. Their women and children had to be sold into slavery. I was appalled.

No one could say whether the Prophet ordered this outrage. He simply turned his face the other way. At the very least that is what he did, and I am here to remind him.

"I am studying the Koran," I tell him. "Does it not say that Islam confirms what came before?"

Muhammad nods.

"Does it not say that God sent down the Torah and after that the Gospels? I see here a sura that compares Jesus to Adam, since they were the only two men who had no earthly father."

Muhammad nods again, giving no sign of how he feels toward me.

I go on, "And yet you drive out the Jews and call them enemies and traitors. Please clear up my confusion, dear master. Are they not also people of the Book?"

I'm saying all this in public, you see. The circle of those who constantly surround him are uncomfortable. For a second the Prophet's eyes flicker in their direction. Is he saying, *If you love me, pluck out this thorn?*

But aloud he is calm and tolerant. "God is all-mighty. He sees all and knows all. He sees those who oppose Him, and they will pay the price. To oppose the faith must mean that someone's heart is set against God, even if their lips pay service to the Book."

His close circle murmurs at the wisdom of his reply. I consider myself lucky to have gotten off with a veiled threat.

Whatever anyone thinks of me, I am never asleep. The day I foresaw came. A year after Badr, the Quraysh mounted a new army and were marching on us. The enemy forces were larger this time and better armed. The gleam of their swords attracted birds from miles around. The enemy were thirsty for revenge. They hadn't forgotten Abu Jahl and all their relatives who were killed alongside him. Muhammad called a council, and since all the chiefs attended, he couldn't exclude me.

The Prophet had the first word. "We shouldn't march out to meet the Quraysh. It is best that we defend the city from within its walls." Knowing how outnumbered we were, I sided with him. This plan displeased the young, restless Muslims. They didn't want to sit at home like women. Their voices cried out for war, which meant marching onto the field. They believed that Allah had given us victory before, and He would protect us now.

Muhammad waited for others to support him, and the older chiefs did. But the clamor for battle was too loud. Two days later, a force of seven hundred left the city. I rode beside the Prophet, and both of us could see in our mind's eye the three thousand Quraysh we were about to meet.

The walls of Medina were still in sight behind us when Muhammad turned to me with a scowl. "Who are those?" he said, pointing to a small band of my soldiers. When I told him they were Jews, some of my truest allies, Muhammad exclaimed, "Back! All of you. We fight without you today."

I was stunned, but my mind didn't quit working. If the Prophet's army won, I would be excluded from God's miracle. If it fell, I would be branded as the reason.

"I want to be with you," I said. Not so much because it was the truth as that I needed another sign of his real motives.

Muhammad's voice softened. "No blame will fall to you. My wishes have been disobeyed already."

Suddenly I read his mind. He wanted my forces to defend the city from within. We were the last resort he had to carry out his plan. I raised my hand and whistled. My lieutenants looked confused, but when I pointed to the city gates, they passed the order along, and we retreated back into Medina.

My men were seen leaving, but not all left. I heard from one of my spies that the two armies had come within sight of each other the first night. Muhammad seized the best ground by making camp on the face of a high hill known as Uhud. The steep rock face at his back protected the troops from being surrounded. Muhammad was in a strong position unless one of his flanks gave way. In that case, the men were both exposed and trapped.

Gazing down from the hillside, Muhammad saw that his soldiers were outnumbered three to one. This didn't alarm him, as he knew the power of faith. In any other war the Muslims would lose; in holy war they would prevail.

The Quraysh were led by Sufyan, the wealthy merchant whose caravan was in peril before the battle at

Badr. He was the wealthiest among the Quraysh, and his money bought them a huge cavalry. They outnumbered Muhammad's cavalry in armored camels fifty to one. Muhammad now heard the songs of women. The Quraysh brought their families with them. They could not be routed without incurring shame. With this news, my spy had nothing more to report. Dawn would tell the tale.

A new spy came running at noon the next day, flush with excitement. "Allah has inspired the Prophet! Nothing can stop him!" Once he calmed down, I questioned him, and the news was stunning. Muhammad, knowing that he had to stop the cavalry from surrounding him, took fifty archers and posted them on a separate low hill. He commanded them to rain arrows down on the Quraysh. On no account were they to rush into battle, not to help their kin or to seize plunder if the enemy was losing.

The Meccan army charged first. Holding their ground on the side of Mount Uhud, the Muslims hurled stones while the archers on their flank shot volleys of arrows. The Quraysh fell back in confusion. In the onrush, their standard fell, and the standard bearer was killed. His brother rushed forward to raise the flag again. Out of the Muslim army Ali stepped forward. Everyone froze. This was the hero of Badr. Ali challenged the new standard bearer to a duel and killed him with the first blow.

Another brother of the standard bearer came out to retrieve the flag, and he too was killed in hand-to-hand combat, followed by his son. Their corpses made a piteous sight. The dueling had devastated Qurayshi morale. Sufyan couldn't rouse them. The war songs of their women and the steely tinkling of bells were but a vain attempt to spur them on.

"And you saw the victory?" I asked my spy.

"No, sir. I ran to tell you, as victory is certain. Allah has inspired the Prophet."

I sent him away. Enough of that. My men, the ones defending the city walls, were in place, tense and waiting. No women sang for them. Everyone was overcome with dread. I could have told them the good news. Instead, I took myself home to ponder fate. The first time Muhammad marched to Medina in triumph, he seized my power. This time, once he accused me of fleeing the battlefield, he'd take my life.

Exhausted, I fell into a troubled sleep. Pounding on the door woke me, and I heard one of my spies shouting for joy. *Is this it? Have all the gods abandoned me?* I secretly thought. But I flung open the door and exclaimed, "Praise Allah!"

Only to see the man's blanched face and the tracks of tears in the dirt on his cheeks.

"Lost!" he cried, sinking to his knees.

I didn't wait for details. If Muhammad had been beaten, that meant three thousand Quraysh mad for vengeance would be laying siege to Medina. I ran to the ramparts to reinforce my men with boys and even women, who could throw stones and pour boiling water on any enemies who tried to climb the city walls.

It's strange when you are about to die and don't know who to pray to. My men were simple. They prayed to Allah with fervent hearts. A handful looked to the sky instead of bowing to earth. I imagined they were praying to the gods of their fathers. As for me, I wouldn't pray until the moment a Qurayshi sword was about to plunge into my chest. I should have had a clear idea at that moment which god wanted me for his own.

And yet the attack never came. Before nightfall a rider appeared on the horizon. I gave permission for the gates to swing open. Once before me, he related a tale I could hardly believe. The battle of Uhud was won. The Muslims killed the enemy's courage, and to save their fallen the Quraysh left camp. Seeing that the spoils of war were in their grasp, the archers couldn't resist. Disobeying Muhammad's orders, they left their post to loot the enemy tents and steal the camels.

A chief on the enemy side, Khalid, the son of Walid, was in charge of their cavalry. He immediately spotted the opening and ordered his troops to charge at the Muslims' exposed flank. Suddenly the crushing weight of their numbers came down on the Muslims. They were surrounded, and their only escape was to retreat uphill on the side of Uhud. In the confusion, the Prophet was set upon and nearly killed before his men could pull him to safety, seriously wounded.

It was the end. All the Quraysh had to do was to pursue the Muslims. But inexplicably, they didn't push forward. The Quraysh allowed Muhammad and his army to escape.

Amazed, I asked, "Where are they now?"

"Coming home," the rider replied, still gasping from distress and fatigue. "See the dust?" He pointed to the horizon, where a line of dirty brown smudged the air.

"Are they running with the Quraysh behind them?"

He shook his head. "The enemy remains in camp. No one pursues us."

How could this be? Perhaps Allah really was on the Prophet's side and had clouded the minds of the enemy. Perhaps Sufyan thought too much like a merchant instead of a general. He didn't want Medina turned into an enemy fortress that would never trade with him again. For whatever reason, the cloud of dust swelled until it reached high overhead. Shrouded inside was the Muslim army, bearing their wounded Prophet home.

Should I move to seize my power back? I wanted to, but my hand was stayed. Too many have converted to Islam. They won't follow an infidel anymore. And there's another thing. Muhammad's God did keep the city from being attacked. It just took a rout to make it happen.

I begged audience with the wounded Prophet to see for myself if he was really alive or on the verge of death. It took two days before I was allowed to enter his room, and by that time he was sitting up in bandages, weak but ready to get strong again.

"What happened?" I asked, keeping my forehead to the floor in case he saw something in my eyes I didn't want seen.

"They disobeyed God," he said grimly. "They stopped fighting for Him."

"Did God tell you that?"

"He didn't have to. Anyone who isn't fighting for God defeats himself."

I felt Muhammad reach down and lift my face from the floor. "Including you," he said. "I would lose any battle to win a great soul."

I can't help now but hear those words over and over. With half my heart I praise Allah sincerely. I'm not the deep-dyed hypocrite they suppose. With the other half of my heart I fear Allah. Perhaps He is all-knowing and all-powerful. Or is He simply crafty beyond imagining?

17.

Umar,
the Close Companion

I t never ended. Skirmishes, feints, raids, and attacks. The struggle was wearing us down. One day the word came that our implacable foe in Mecca, Abu Sufyan, had taken the profits of a whole caravan to buy weapons and mercenaries. Everything was closing in. The next day we heard that the hill stronghold of Taif would resist Islam to the last man. Syria refused peace terms, inflamed by lies about the Prophet. The Bedouin chiefs on the coast drifted from our side to the Meccans like waves on the beach.

And yet he goes on. A recent revelation comes to his lips: "Allah taxes not one soul beyond its limits."

I am *sahabi*, one of the companions who has been by the Prophet's side since the beginning. No one has kept a closer eye on him. Closeness doesn't reveal his secrets, though. One waits for clues, like watching a lion who seems to sleep and then gives one small twitch before he leaps. A few months ago there was a lull in the raids and killings and betrayals. I found the Prophet kneeling in his garden. At first I hung back, so that I wouldn't interrupt his prayers. He looked up and beckoned me.

"Watch," he said, pointing at the ground.

A small anthill lay in front of him. Carefully the Prophet put a balled-up piece of bread next to it. At first only one or two ants came out to scout. They touched the bread with their feelers, then scurried back inside. In a minute dozens of ants trickled out to pick at the dropped food. I must admit I found nothing unusual to see. The Prophet was brandishing a twig, which he used to gently push the ants away. Every time he did this, more ants rushed out of the ground to fill in the gap.

"This is our situation," he murmured. "No matter how many enemies we drive away, more are sent after them." He cocked his head quizzically at me. "What would you have me do? The faithful can't face attack forever."

"Do you want me to show you?" I asked in return. He nodded. With my sandal I kicked the anthill, sending it flying. I stamped on the flattened ground, and the hole disappeared. The ants around the bread ball scattered in confusion.

"If God wants us to fight our enemies, then He wants us to crush them. Mount a massive attack," I said. "Every Muslim in creation will rush to fight. Do nothing, and the Quraysh will gather more allies, like flies to rotting meat." On the wind we had heard of powerful tribes that were being bought off by Mecca with promises of plunder. The banished Jewish tribes were constantly trading with the enemy and nursing their dark grievances.

The Prophet picked up an ant on his fingertip and examined it. "Tomorrow more will come out of the ground. You can't kill them all."

"I can kill enough. I can kill until Allah tells me to stop."

I had worked myself half into a rage, but the Prophet gazed at the destroyed anthill in sorrow. "God has something better in mind," he murmured.

"Better than total victory?"

The Prophet turned away and went back into the house. That's what I mean about getting a clue to his mind. When you glimpse one, it is veiled. In the short run, events turned out the way I foresaw, but it was Mecca that mounted the massive attack, not us. It was in the spring two years after Uhud. This time the Quraysh were preparing for a long siege against Medina. Word came of ten thousand infantry led by a cavalry of six hundred horses. Our army was a third that size. Brave Muslims went to bed only to wake up wide-eyed, because they heard the clang of iron horseshoes in their nightmares.

My nightmare was just as horrifying, but more real. When we were routed at Uhud, it took every fiber of strength to remove the wounded Prophet safely from the field. Trailing behind the retreat, I glanced over my shoulder. With shrill war cries the camp followers from Mecca had rushed onto the bloody ground, maiming and mutilating the fallen. They were human vultures, and the leader wasn't a savage, but Hind, the wife of Sufyan himself. I wonder if she spied me, because her face was like a demon's. I saw her raise a small curved blade, and when she brought it down, a wounded Muslim had lost his nose and ears. Sickened, I turned and galloped away. Later I heard that some women returned to Mecca wearing necklaces of body parts sliced from the dead and dying.

Rumblings spread through the city after that defeat. It took all of the Prophet's skill to calm the bickering chieftains. One bitter faction wanted to punish the reckless young warriors who had ignored the Prophet's plan to defend Medina. There was even more disgust over the archers who had abandoned their post to loot the enemy camp. But the Prophet said quietly, "All that

is good comes from Allah. All that is ill is my fault."
His humility swayed the chieftains, even as blood was
shed among clans in Medina's back streets at night.

We gathered in council to argue about how to meet
the massive army marching toward us. Spies had ridden
ahead to warn us that we had only a week to prepare.
The worst confusion is that born of panic. The Prophet
sat silently, while the chieftains tore apart each other's
plans. One side shouted that Badr had been won by hitting the enemy full on and trusting in Allah. A quieter,
more cautious faction pointed out that staying home to
defend Medina from the inside would have avoided the
humiliating defeat at Uhud.

The Prophet turned to the quiet faction. "You do
not call upon God to bring us victory?"

"I would thank God if He brought us survival," one
of the chiefs muttered.

The Prophet grew stern. "Where is your faith?" But
he knew well enough that there was near famine already in the city. Reciters roamed the streets crying out
verses from the Koran to raise morale. People listened,
but continued to tremble.

I stood up among the assembly. "The Prophet has
taught us that faith has three parts. One part lies in the
heart, another in our words, and the last in our deeds.
Every action is holy. Therefore, this must be a holy

battle, not a battle of fear. We should rejoice in being tested."

Maybe I raised a few sunken hearts with this kind of boldness. But we all knew that there was a fourth part of faith, and it belonged only to the Prophet, the one man who could hear directly from God. We waited in nervous, rustling silence. He rose to his feet.

"Our enemies fight against God, and therefore they are defeated in advance. Not knowing this, they assemble a great, futile army. But ten thousand blind men cannot defeat a handful who can see. Let me ask you, then, what do you see? If you tell me that you see a foe who hopelessly outnumbers us, then are you not as blind as they?"

A mixture of bafflement and discontent greeted these words. A voice cried out, "Tell us what you see."

The Prophet shrugged. "I took a walk out of town yesterday. I saw hills and rocks and trees the same as you. But this time God showed them to me with new eyes, and I rejoiced." He smiled beatifically. "Is it not wonderful how God brings us victory in His very creation?"

The assembly was more baffled than ever by his words. A few of the *sahabi* who knew him well realized he was about to unveil a teaching.

"Allah is all-merciful. He asks nothing of our souls except what he has already planted in them," Muhammad raised his voice to silence the muttering doubters. "I will give you a plan, but never forget my words. *God is all-merciful.* This is worth more than victory, more than life itself."

Muhammad explained how the rocks, hills, and trees that he loved to walk among surrounded the city on three sides. An army couldn't march through them without being picked off; horses couldn't gallop through without losing their footing. Medina had only one open side, to the north. If we could stop the enemy's horses there, they would lose most of their advantage. The tide would swing to us, because the Qurayshi infantry knew that in hand-to-hand combat a Muslim protected by his faith was worth three mercenaries fighting for loot.

"Their warhorses have seen bloodshed. They won't run from the glint of steel or the clash of swords," said the Prophet. "So we must give them something they've never seen before. Only the unknown can frighten a warhorse."

By this time the assembly was hanging on to his every word. I don't know if God enjoys creating suspense; if the Prophet does, it's a small sin. "What we need is simplicity itself. It is written that long ago the Persians terrified the enemy by digging a deep trench in the front lines. If the walls are steep enough, no horse will plunge into such a trench. They will pull up short at the last moment in panic. We will defend ourselves against the siege by fighting from behind our trenches."

This strategy was delivered so skillfully that no one had time to consider the vast labor it would take to dig a single ditch deeper than a horse is tall, even when only on the north side of the city. The enemy army would be upon us in seven days, which meant that we had a mere six days to prepare our fortifications.

I tell you, those six days were the noblest of my life. Medina worked with one back, digging night and day. Every child was given a shovel to work beside his father. Women hauled away dirt in baskets and took turns bringing food and water. The Prophet himself was seen digging, his white robes dirtied, his face caked with dust. All the better to goad our men to dig until their arms burned and trembled with exhaustion.

As I was breaking my back, my heart repeated encouraging words given by God in His book:

Lo, I swear by the afterglow of sunset,
And by the night and all that it enshrouds,
And by the moon when she is at the full,
You will journey to higher and higher worlds.

Wasn't I doing that now? To mortal eyes I was no more than a sweaty soldier squeezed into a ditch beside a thousand other soldiers. Yet in my soul I was working toward a higher world. Nothing stronger can drive a man onward. When I fell into bed at night, I dreamed of Paradise. No more did the horrifying sight of women mutilating fallen bodies trouble me.

The Prophet surveyed the work, sending in fresh replacements when a section of the trench fell behind. The fierceness of the task seemed to please him.

Legends were already circulating about him, and I remembered one. The Prophet has a large band of horses that he loves. Being a child of the desert, he grew up with Bedouins, who took their favorite mares inside the tent with them at night, for fear that raiders would steal them while they slept.

One day the Prophet had run his horses far out into the sands without water. In the distance an oasis came in sight. The animals were desperately thirsty; they bolted toward the oasis as soon as they smelled it. The Prophet watched them run away. At the last moment before they reached water, he rose in his stirrups and gave a sharp whistle, signaling for them to come back.

Most of the horses ignored the whistle, but five mares turned and returned to his hand. These alone he selected for breeding. He said, "A horse can be whipped into running faster. With discipline it can be made to fight in battle. But what God values is complete loyalty, and that appears only when a soul meets the sorest test."

You see? We were loyal mares in a moment of desperation, which is why the fiercer the danger, the happier he grew.

Finally the horizon was filled with black specks that advanced under a thin brown layer of dust. The specks grew into human shapes, and in less than a day the ranks of foot soldiers, cavalry, and fighters on camels filled our vision. The siege began. We had made life harder for the invaders by harvesting the crops early and stripping the land of forage. The Prophet emptied the city of men and boys over fifteen, stationing them on the hill above the trench. No one was allowed to go home at night; all were ordered to pray in loud voices and to spread out their campfires in long lines to make the Quraysh believe that there were more of us than there were.

At the first charge the enemy was dumbfounded. Their horses were afraid to plunge into the trench, and when a few hotheads forced them to try and leap across, they fell short and tumbled to the bottom, writhing and whinnying in panic. After that, there was no second charge. For two weeks neither side moved. Ali killed one of their leaders in a duel. Otherwise, the casualties were one or two a day. Seeing this, the Prophet should have been encouraged, but he sat for hours in gloomy reflection.

I went to cheer him up, and myself. The whole future rested on his mood. "How can I be happy?" he said. "God has granted us everything, but He can't change human nature, not in a week, and among sinners perhaps not ever."

He suspected betrayals, and the longer the siege lasted, the more tempting it was for the hypocrites and unbelievers to turn against us. The nights grew colder; rain grayed the skies. I was sent underground, and a day later I returned with ominous news.

"They've found enough traitors to attack us from within. I crawled to within twenty yards of the tents where the bargaining is going on. Already the people know. Rumors are flying everywhere that our women and children will be kidnapped at night while the men are on the barricades."

The Prophet listened as I unfolded my grim report. The key traitors were the Banu Qurayza, the last Jewish tribe in Medina to hold a peace pact with the Muslims. The others had all been banished.

The Prophet's eyes looked troubled. "What is the enemy saying to make the Jews betray us?" He raised his hand. "Don't tell me. The slightest word would be enough."

He knew that the banished Jews had joined the enemy. A few of them came to the Qurayza and laid out the certainty that a vast army couldn't be resisted forever. One enemy emissary, a powerful chief from Khaybar, where many Jews had fled to repair their fortunes, threw open the tent flap of the Qurayza chief.

"What do you see?" the emissary asked. "Nothing but our forces, mile after mile. Yet it will take the whim of just one man, Muhammad, to wipe you out, if his God orders him to. Doesn't he already preach that Jews and Christians should abandon their faith and be converted?"

The emissary chose the right poison. The Qurayza wavered. What side did they want to be on when Medina fell? Up to that point, the pact with the Prophet had been honored on both sides. In return for remaining neutral, the remaining Jews in Medina had sent baskets and tools for digging the trenches.

By then the siege had become a battle of nerves. Every day the two sides stood close enough to hurl insults at each other, but far enough apart that arrows couldn't reach them. Food shortages hurt both camps. The rain and cold eroded morale. In the tensest hour we got news that the Qurayza had torn up the treaty with us. They would open up the city's southern flank, which they controlled, and once that happened, the trench on the north would be useless. Worse than useless, since the men stationed there all day and night had grown exhausted.

I sat in council with the trusted couriers who brought this news to the Prophet. Quietly he gave two orders. "Tell no one that the Qurayza have turned, or there will be panic in the streets. Bring several hundred soldiers and their horses into the center of town, to defend the women and children from attack."

The situation was dire. Muhammad turned to the Ghatafan, a nomadic tribe who had recently ignited the wrath of the Muslims, first by joining the Quraysh and lending them a major contingent of fighters and arms, but also by their relentless greed. God told the Prophet that he must break the alliance of his enemies. Looking to the weakest link, he landed upon the Ghatafan, because they could be bought off. The Prophet offered them a third of the date harvest if they abandoned the war.

This was an excessive offer as far as Ali and the other fighters were concerned, but then the Ghatafan spat in our faces, demanding not a third but half the year's crop as their bribe. At that moment God spoke in a mystifying way. He told the Prophet to agree. This decision was greeted with stunned silence.

I was made deputy and ordered to take the agreement to the Ghatafan chiefs. It was a degrading mission, and my heart was heavy. Before I left, I went to the Prophet's tent to make sure that this was his will. He nodded silently. As I was leaving, though, he said in a mild voice, "Out of respect, show the agreement to the Muslim chiefs." It seemed like no more than a casual reminder.

I went to the stronghold in the center of town where the Muslim chiefs had gathered for safety. When I presented them with the parchment on which the agreement was inked, they flew into a rage and tore it up. The Prophet was shamed in many eyes, and defeat, it seemed, had gotten one day closer with the Ghatafan still against us.

When everyone had disbanded in great discouragement, the Prophet kept me behind. "Remember the anthill you stamped out in a rage?" he asked. "Do you still think you can kill them all?"

I hung my head.

"I am not shaming you, dear friend," he murmured. "But do you also recall that I held a single ant on my fingertip?"

I nodded. "Did that mean something?"

The Prophet smiled. "Not then. But God has now brought me the key to victory, and it's a single ant."

As I stared in amazement, he explained. During the previous night, Nuaym, an elder of the Ghatafan tribe, had sneaked across enemy lines. He demanded to see the Prophet, but was turned away with insults. Nuaym persevered until eventually he came into the Prophet's holy presence. The two met in secret, and when Nuaym departed, the Prophet was wreathed in smiles.

"God tests me with an army of ants, but then He sends me the only one who matters."

Unknown to anyone, it turns out, Nuaym had become a Muslim convert. He could circulate freely among all the enemy factions and was trusted by them. He now began to sow discord as the Prophet secretly instructed him.

To the Qurayza, Nuaym said, "Before you switch sides to the Quraysh, consider this. If they lose this battle, they will march home and abandon you. Ask for some hostages among their chiefs in exchange for your cooperation. If you've picked the right side, all is well. If you haven't, you can ransom the hostages to Muhammad for your own safe release."

The Qurayza thanked him for his counsel and sent word to the Quraysh that they needed hostages before agreeing to anything. Nuaym was there when the demand arrived. To the Meccans he whispered, "Why do they want hostages from their protectors? It can only be to trade them to Muhammad the minute they are turned over."

Both sides believed him, and the next time they met, it was with narrowed eyes and suspicious minds. The Quraysh refused to give hostages. The Qurayza refused to fight against the Muslims, falling back on neutrality as their best hope. God saw other, more hidden weaknesses among the enemy. Wherever Nuaym went, he found it easy to open old wounds and festering distrust. Never had one ant wreaked so much havoc.

The wind blew strong that night. Standing on the city walls, I could see the enemy's campfires winking out. Hosts of soldiers would sleep fitfully on the cold ground without a fire. *If God isn't doing this to them, who do they think is?* But I never expected to witness the sight that greeted us at dawn—an empty field where thousands had been camped the day before. It was as if the angel Gabriel had descended and swept the ground clean. The foe left behind their wounded horses and camels, whose pitiful groans were carried to us on the same wind that had blown the enemy back to Mecca.

I fell at the Prophet's feet. "It's a miracle!" I exclaimed.

But he shook his head. "Only a few, like Abu Sufyan, deeply hate us. The rest came for plunder. The weakest reed flattens before the wind."

Actually, the ones who truly needed a miracle were the Qurayza, who had no protection now against the wrath of the Muslim hordes that descended on them, crying traitor. The Jews retreated to their stronghold and held out bravely. After almost a month, when starvation threatened their existence, they held council. Three outcomes would end the siege. They could convert to Islam and renounce all ties to their Jewish God. As a second choice, they could murder their wives and children, giving themselves no reason to live, and launch a suicide attack on the Muslims. Finally, they could pretend to observe the Sabbath and turn the day into a surprise attack. None of these alternatives was acceptable, though, which left total surrender as the only possibility. The Qurayza straggled out to meet their fate.

The crowd was hungry for blood. What was the Prophet to do with the traitors? He chose a course no one expected. "Let there be a judge who has nothing to gain by his judgment." The man he chose was Sa'd ibn Mua'dh, who was no more than a well-respected trader. But when the name was announced, the mob gasped and drew back as he was dragged into the public square on a litter wrapped in bloody sheets. Sa'd had fought at the trench and received a wound from which he was slowly dying. On all sides it was agreed that such a man had no stake in any judgment. The Jewish captives took heart, because Sa'd was their former ally. Law and custom bound him to them, even if they had done ill to anyone else.

The Prophet withdrew, declaring that the judge's rendering would be final. The Qurayza pleaded for leniency, offering all their worldly goods and their women and children as slaves if their lives could be spared. Other allies kneeled before Sa'd and joined in the cries for mercy. For all the anxiety and panic they had caused, the Qurayza had never formally joined the enemy.

Sa'd listened as his bandages oozed. He was gray and weak. In a croaking voice he spoke his decision, and I ran to deliver it to the Prophet.

"Death to all the men. Slavery for the women and children." It was the harshest possible sentence. The Prophet made no comment except to order that the executioners should come from every tribe in Medina. This would assure that no single one would take the blame and all would share the guilt. Over four hundred Jews were bound and lost their heads. The Prophet received no revelation about sparing them or killing them, either way. He became stoic and grim. After the tension of the siege, he seemed to retreat into himself even more, and what time he spent in company was almost always with his wives, especially Aisha, the youngest, who had risen in his favor.

Months later I took her aside. "What does he really think of the judgment?" I asked.

Aisha said nothing, but she must have run to the Prophet. The next day, when he saw me hanging back during prayers, he said, "Walk with me."

I obeyed, keeping quiet. I have the stomach for any battle, but the blood of the Qurayza was another thing.

"Do you have a question?" the Prophet asked after we had reached a cool stand of trees in the woods.

I hesitated. "Do I have a right to question?"

"A good answer. Allah is to be feared. He is also to be loved. From one moment to the next, I cannot be sure which He wants. Do you understand?"

"I'm not sure." I wasn't sliding under the question. The Prophet was talking about doubt, and yet he taught that doubt would destroy us faster than any enemy.

He said, "God does not hand down the truth all at once. He hands it down the way a wildflower scatters its seed, sending it in all directions. Life brings a thousand situations, and there must be a truth for each one." The Prophet glanced sideways at me. "Can you begin to understand?"

"I think so. For every moment there is a revelation. What is true one time isn't always true the next."

"Yes. But if peace is true today and war tomorrow, how are the faithful to live? The choice cannot be left up to each of us. We are weak and blind. We are corrupted by sin. What should we do?"

I thought of the tale I had heard. "We can run when God whistles."

The Prophet gave the first smile I had seen in a month. "You may abhor his judgment, but Sa'd gave me hope."

"By killing God's enemies?"

"No. To one who loves this life, any death is a reason to mourn. Sa'd could have sided with his tribe. That was the easy way and the way every Arab has known forever. He didn't. He sided with his soul, for he told me afterward that he couldn't face his Creator if he allowed those who hate Allah to go free.

"Do you see the spark of hope? When a man can decide life or death not because he wants revenge, but because he has thoughts of God, human nature is changing. I thought that was impossible, or that it might take twenty generations. By the grace of Allah, we are seeing it in our lifetime."

I listened. I understood. I accepted. In my heart, however, I thought only one human had really changed—him. The Prophet has become his revelations. He sees beyond life and death, and his mind cares only to be part of God's mind. As for the rest of us, we will stamp out anthills for a long time to come.

18.

Yasmin,
the Woman at the Well

O nly once since I was born have I been soaked to the skin. Black clouds moved toward Medina from the hills. Usually they disappoint. I see wisps of rain that stop in midair and never reach the earth. On that day, though, the day the promise was made, thunder cracked overhead like a blacksmith's hammer. It rained so hard that rivers ran down the street.

I would have hidden in a doorway until the storm passed, but something arose in me that I couldn't fight. I ran out into the downpour, stomping in the muddy water until it splashed up to my waist and stained my shift brown. The other women at the well looked at me as if I was crazy.

I was inspired, not crazy. You'll understand, if not now, then soon.

When the downpour ended, I dragged myself back to my little room. It has no windows, so I had to open the door to let in light. I stood in the doorway pulling off my dress, which was so heavy with water that I could hardly lift it over my head. A modest woman would never stand there naked, open to men's eyes. Modesty is a luxury I couldn't afford.

When you live on the streets you get devoured one way or another. I would be dead except for the shelter of that suffocating little room. It was added to the back of my brother's house.

When my brother came to the well and took me by the hand, I was amazed. You see, he had been content to let me starve. And then suddenly and without a word he led me to his house.

"You can't come in. My wife won't have a woman like you inside. Your place is in the back."

I gave him a baffled look, and he said, "Don't ask me why. It's a gift from Allah."

I'm grateful. I don't ask why Allah couldn't have added a window. But with certain men, as they grope and grab, darkness is a blessing. One day a different sort came to the back.

This man was young and nervous. From his accent I could tell he was a Bedouin, just in from the country. I told him to sit on the bed; I knelt and began to remove his sandals.

"Don't," he mumbled.

Just then the last ray of sunlight peeked through a crack in the door, and I saw a tiny red glow, as if a spark had dropped from the sky and landed on his head. A second later the glow was gone.

When the young man didn't move, I took his hand and placed it on my breast. He snatched it away. I asked him what the matter was. He hesitated, saying nothing, and I held my breath. He was nice-looking. His beard curled at the corners, which gave him a whimsical look, like a poet. I don't lie down with many poets. I felt under the mattress for the dagger I keep there. Nice looks are no guarantee that he hadn't come to rob me. Then his hand wandered back to my breast. He moaned softly, and I relaxed.

Nature would have taken its sweaty course, but I hadn't pulled the door tight enough. There was a small crack to let in the sound of the call to evening prayer. The moment he heard it, the young man jumped to his feet with a startled cry. A Muslim, like my brother. He unrolled a small rug that he was carrying on his back and knelt to the floor.

Not that I could really see him in the dark. I heard him saying the words, in a soft mumble. "Praise be to Allah, the Lord of creation, the compassionate, the merciful."

"So God is more important to you than love?" I asked, watching him from the bed.

"God is more important than life," he said. I wondered if my mocking tone would make him hit me. Yet quite the opposite happened. He sat beside me and began to weep. I didn't know what to do. Something about his tears touched me.

"Lie down," I said soothingly. "We don't have to do anything, but if you want, I can teach you about love."

I felt his neck stiffen under my fingers. "Love? You're just a common—" He caught himself and stopped.

"Perhaps not so common. You haven't given me a chance." I hadn't eaten that day. It would be a shame to lose the few coins he'd pay.

The young man roughly pushed my hand away. He got up and went for the door. Instead of leaving, though, he stood there a moment, pulling at his ear. He thrust something tiny and sharp into my palm.

"Keep this. I will return one day for it, and then I will teach you about love."

In a second he was gone. I opened my hand. How amazing. In the candlelight I saw a small perfect ruby. It was shaped like a teardrop and set into an earring. So that was the red spark that had shone in the dark. I could hardly sleep that night thinking about the curly-haired young man.

The next day I caught a glimpse of him. I wore the earring brazenly to the well. Its shine would attract the eyes of more men. But as it turned out, nobody had time for me. Soldiers were milling about the square. They were infantry mixed in tight with horses and camels. So tight that when I caught a glimpse of my young man, I couldn't press my way to reach him. He turned his head away before our eyes met. I cried out, but the din was too great. Then some busybody got the other women to shout "Slut!" because they thought I was there to grab a holy warrior, a *mujahid*, for myself.

With a clatter of arms and followed by loud cries, the *mujahidin* marched off, and the square grew quiet. I stood apart, in the corner under a half-dead palm tree reserved for my kind. My finger went to my ear and I touched the ruby my soldier had given me. *My soldier?* He hadn't even touched me except over my shift. And yet I couldn't get him out of my head. His memory didn't comfort me. Every day got more lonely instead. I lay in the dark kissing the ruby as if he was there, and the last words I heard were, "When I return, I will teach you about love."

My passion grew like a coal fanned by the wind. I couldn't tell anyone. I made up my mind to ready myself before the army came home. They had marched far away to Syria. It would be days or weeks. God's reach is far, and he rewards any man who fights for him. My soldier would drop gold at my feet and then he would marry me. I know a whore's logic is worth less than the ridicule it takes to scorn it. In secret, I followed the reciters around the streets. They have taken up the Koran as their stock-in-trade. People listen hypnotized. They say that the best reciters make strong men weep and convert infidels on the spot.

As for me, I didn't weep for God. Not at first. I wept for my soldier; a strong trembling came over me when I thought of him. Even so, the calls to prayer no longer irritated me. They felt comforting, like a faraway voice calling to me. I knew what I had to do.

The day it poured down rain was the day I knew something must change. The rain was a sign and the joy I felt a path toward something yet to be uncovered. After I dried off, I reached under my bed for the small bag of silver coins I had saved up over many years. I bought myself a modest dress and veil. I locked my door against the men. The only course left was begging. I went to the well and looked the other women in the eye.

"I want to repent. Help me save my soul. Whatever dirty chore you want done, give it to me. It doesn't matter how menial or filthy."

They stared, those who would stoop to look at me. But one old woman heard something in my voice. She took pity and led me to her house. We scrubbed the floor on our knees together. Her stiff joints wouldn't let her do the work alone. After that, when she was certain that God wouldn't strike her dead for bringing impurity to her home, she asked me back. She had cousins, and after a while I cleaned latrines and picked nits out of children's hair. I became known for my willingness to do things only a slave would do. It helped when I entered a house and recognized one of the men. They were eager to hire me if I kept my mouth shut.

The old lady was named Halimah, and God must have sent her. Not only did she hire me, but she had been the wet nurse to Muhammad. Old age had brought her out of the desert, and she followed the Prophet to Medina.

"He saw his first angels when he was with me. Two of them, who reached into his heart, and he wasn't seven yet," she said.

After that, I became eager for more. I had glimpsed Muhammad in the streets. Everyone did. As he passed by, he was like a shadow. I never knew he talked to angels. His old nurse wasn't ready to reveal anything, not just yet.

"I still smell what you were, and it's too early to see what you might become," she said leaving me to my scrubbing.

Then one day Halimah offered to walk me back to my room. We said nothing on the way, until a rich man's house came into view. To one side stood a gazebo where the family took the cool evening air. Halimah stopped and gazed at it. A graceful white dome was held up by pillars carved from twisted wood to imitate vines.

"I've never had time to rest, and no one has ever invited me inside such a lovely place," the old lady said quietly.

"Are you jealous?" I asked.

"You mean, do I feel the way you do? No." She cocked her head in my direction. "The dome of heaven is held up by five pillars. I own them. Here." She touched her heart, but instead of explaining she rushed on. We parted at my corner. I suppose my little room also smelled too much of who I was.

News of the Syrian campaign reached Medina. The Muslim force had been savagely attacked without warning. Someone had warned the emperor's deputy in Damascus, and the Byzantines were ready. There was a bloody skirmish. Many were lost. I heard all this in scraps as the wind carried the words from the well, where the women looked anxious and afraid. I was afraid too. It wasn't just his presence that I longed for. There was something else, and I didn't understand how to find it. I told Halimah that I was growing desperate. Then she surprised me.

"I already knew that. I felt your desperation before you did."

"How?"

I looked up. She was standing over me, straightening out her creaky knees.

"The wage of sin is desperation," she said. There was no sermon that followed. Instead she taught me to pray, my face to the floor, facing toward Mecca because God's house was there. She gave me the same prayer I had heard my soldier mumble. "Praise be to Allah, the Lord of creation, the compassionate, the merciful." I was glad for that.

Halimah warned me that I must pray at exactly the appointed hours of the day when the muezzin called, and then one last time before I went to bed. I nodded, wrung the last drops of water from my scrubbing rag, and started to leave.

Halimah shook her head. "You haven't asked why we pray."

I blushed. I couldn't tell her that I was praying for a soldier whose name I didn't even know.

"We pray out of gratitude to God. He has given us everything. Remember that, child." She caught a look in my eyes. "You don't believe me. Because you think God hasn't given you much."

I didn't dare speak or even nod. If she sent me away, I'd have no more work or bread.

"Let me tell you what you are," she said.

My heart sank. "I thought that you, of all people, wouldn't tell me." I heard my voice shake.

Halimah took my hand. "Listen to me, my dear. You are not what you seem. You are God's child. Fate has taken you far away from Him to show you what it is like to be lost. But it's the will of God to bring you back, all the more to rejoice."

Something inside me cracked. I trembled like a virgin stripped naked before a stranger. Halimah and I wept together, and that was the start. I learned what I must do to deserve God's grace. I prayed, a reminder in thought and word that God is here. The world pulls us away; the voice of sin is never silent. But if we re- member God throughout the day, our souls approach his glory.

I followed Halimah around and watched her. She wrapped up pieces of bread and thrust small coins into each one. These she gave to the street beggars. That's how I learned to remember the poor, as the Koran tells us. It was autumn, and when Ramadan came, Halimah sat in her room for most of the day. I brought her a tray of food, but she barely touched it or the jug of water I put by her bed. She didn't have to tell me that she was fasting, or that the Koran told her to, but I had to know why.

"For a month we remember who we are," she said. "We are not this body that is nourished by food and water. We are made for God, and so it is right to repent of the flesh, and to abstain from the flesh's craving."

She smiled like a child. "Of course, there are cravings I gave up long ago. We won't speak of that."

Her simplicity moved me. Halimah trusted me. I was welcome in her house without suspicion or scorn. Nothing was locked away from me. So it was an easy step to accept her trust in God.

As for my soldier, he never returned. The *mujahidin* marched home. The calamity of the Byzantine attack was written on their faces. They dragged the corpses of the fallen behind them, wrapped in white winding sheets. I couldn't look. If my soldier was one of them, it would be unbearable. Halimah noticed, of course, but she didn't say anything when she found me weeping in a corner.

One day when I came to scrub the floors, she surprised me with a table spread out for a guest.

"Why didn't you tell me I shouldn't come?" I asked.

"Why should I? You are the guest."

I had never seen lamb and apricots in her larder before, and the fresh oil she dripped over the soft warm bread smelled like an orchard in spring.

"What's this for?" I asked. I couldn't imagine where she found the money, and suddenly a pang of worry struck me. Perhaps this was her leave-taking. Was the old woman ready to die?

Instead of answering me, Halimah said, "Which is better, to dream of a feast or to eat it?"

"To eat it," I replied mechanically.

Halimah passed me a platter of shredded lamb steamed in spiced rice. "It's time you realized that."

It took me time to understand her teaching. For that moment, I was just glad to be her guest. In the past hunger had been my constant companion during the month of Ramadan, which had just ended. Muslims led such quiet lives then that there were almost no calls for me. Halimah stopped eating long before I was full, but she was content to watch me. When I took my sleeve and wiped the last bit of lamb grease from my mouth, she smiled.

"Now the feast begins."

Halimah looked amused at my puzzlement. "When the body has had enough, the mind still craves its own feast. So far, you have been satisfied with wishes. You dream of being as full here"—she touched her heart—"as you are here." She moved her hand to her stomach. "But as you said, it's better to eat a feast than to dream of one. Are you ready?"

"I don't know." Her words made me a little frightened.

She went on. "You are standing at the door for the first time. What lies ahead is dim. But the angel who came to the Prophet speaks to you. He speaks on the wind and among the stars. Who knows what the wind says? The space between the stars is silent. That is why we have the Koran. The angel's message lives in the Book. Anyone can understand it.

"The world has unfolded according to God's will. There have been many prophets and messengers. But men soon forget, and then God sends those who warn of danger. Men still turn their backs, and finally God sends the pure word of truth. When that happens, there is no excuse. This is the golden hour."

She had memorized scraps of the Koran, and with a glowing face she murmured one now. "Call on Him with fear and longing in your heart, for the mercy of God is near to those who do good."

A silence fell between us. "Fear?" I said. "Why must I call on God in fear?"

"Because your young soldier may be dead. I'm sure you have other fears. Who else will ease them for you?"

Halimah had never mentioned him before, and I had no idea how she knew. I pulled my veil over my face to spare her the stricken look that came over me. "Can God bring back the dead?" I whispered.

"If He wills it, yes. But that isn't the point." Halimah's voice grew sharper, as if she was pulling me back to myself. "To be born is to suffer, and to sin. The Arabs take no notice of mercy. Life is harder here than anywhere else. There is no better place to forget God than the desert. What is the point of suffering, but to endure?

"Then one day God put Gabriel, his most trusted angel, in a small boat. He placed the Koran in his hands, and the little boat set sail. It arrived at the shores of Arabia, and you know what the angel said? 'This hard land has made hard hearts. I will find one man who will heed God's word. I will stand by him every day, giving him drops of truth the way a mother gives a squalling babe drops of milk. In time, these hard hearts will melt.'"

I will never forget that day, nor the teaching that came with it. Halimah taught me that the angel is near, and wherever he goes, a feast is spread.

I became devout and stopped longing for my soldier. After a while others noticed the change. I was given a place at the well, and eventually some asked me my name.

"Yasmin," I said.

I smile now as the black clouds roll in from the hills. The wisps of rain that hang from their bellies tell my story before I let mercy into my heart.

Even so, I do run with the other women to the gates whenever the *mujahidin* return. They go farther and farther these days. The world is ready to fall to its knees. It's time. And I confess it—I search the face of each soldier.

Last month I lay in bed and the door opened. Hearing the hinges creak, I shut my eyes tight. Fate is a guest who can never be turned away.

A man's face brushed my cheek before his hands touched me. I imagined I felt curls in his beard.

"I've come back for the ruby," he whispered. "Didn't I promise?"

My heart beat so fast I thought I would die. "You promised to teach me about love. But I already know."

"There is always more to learn."

I felt his hand plucking the ruby earring from my ear. He held it up, and although it was midnight, the stone began to glow like a spark from heaven. With a sudden plunge he brought the ruby down hard on my chest, and I felt it sink beneath the flesh. It sank as far as my heart. Amazingly, I could still see it. The red glow spread until every chamber of my heart was filled and grew still.

The hinges creaked again, and he was gone. Did I dream it? No one could ever make me believe that. I carry the jewel of redemption in my heart, and with every fiber of my being I know that my soldier had returned for me.

19.
Abu Sufyan,
the Enemy

I call it canny politics. The superstitious call it magic. If you want, you can call it the hand of God. But before he suddenly died last year, Muhammad achieved total victory. He could no more be stopped by force than you can stop a sandstorm by holding up your fist.

Mecca had no choice but to surrender. I will tell you that part in a moment. Many said the Prophet was inviolate from harm. I half believed it myself. My whole body trembled when I was brought before him, like a captive ready for sentencing. Muhammad wasn't the picture of a conqueror. He was subdued. His eyes barely saw me. Where were they fixed—on another world, another revelation? Quietly he said, "I am home again. I bear no ill will. If you wish to join us, the past is the past."

"Wish" was a nice word, a gentle word. He could afford to be gentle with a thousand swords holding the streets of Mecca.

More than anything he had wanted Mecca. To an orphan boy it was still the center of the world. Without it, Muhammad's conquests would have been like a necklace without the priceless pearl. After ten years of strife, though, how could he conquer Mecca when the Quraysh had sworn blood revenge? He would do it God's way, the only way we couldn't fight against.

It took him three years and began with a dream. Muhammad saw himself with his head shaved, the way pilgrims look after they perform the Hajj in Mecca. When he told about his dream, his advisers were shocked. The Hajj belonged to the old religion before Islam. Everyone knows that. How could their new God share the same rites as the old gods? For once Muhammad's followers resisted him. The young *jihadis* who had grown strong in battle were stubborn. Muhammad could not convince them to bend, but finally he let the people in the streets know about his vision.

A clamor arose to return to Mecca. The desire had been sleeping in the exiles' breasts all along. See what I mean about canny politics? A peaceful pilgrimage would bring the exiles home and at the same time reassure us in Mecca that our holy sites wouldn't go bankrupt. They were our lifeblood. After all, each turn around the Kaaba by the pilgrims was like an ox drawing water from a well. We needed it to survive.

And so the Muslims came, wrapped in the white linen skirt and shawl of the devout, dragging hundreds of sacrificial animals and keeping their weapons out of sight. I paid for a band of cavalry led by our best fighter, Khalid, to intercept them. Unfortunately, they completely lost Muhammad's train, which had purposely veered off onto a different, rockier route.

Sitting in council, half the Qurayshi elders wanted to concede. "Let them enter and worship. The Kaaba will still be ours. Doesn't that signal that we have won?"

I stood up trying not to ridicule such feeble logic. "If you let them into Mecca, you are saying that Muhammad is your equal, each one of you. In place of the tribe, which has held us together from the time of Abraham, an upstart will unite the Arabs according to his revelations. Trust me, the first revelation will be to destroy the idols."

Enough elders were persuaded by me that Muhammad had to stop outside the city. When forcibly stopped, he reached out to negotiate. No matter how different Islam is from the faith of our fathers, one thing is agreed upon. The sacred precincts of Mecca cannot be a place for violence. Pilgrims cannot fight holy wars. Holy grace depends upon it.

When his emissaries sued for peace, I didn't relent easily. I forced the chiefs to demand that the Muslims go away for one year before attempting to worship in the city. In return, we would halt hostilities against them for ten years. I know the concession was too great. I was admitting military defeat. But the soldiers of Mecca—every citizen, in fact—believed that the Muslims fought with special magic to protect them. When that kind of belief takes hold, the enemy has won before the first blow has been struck.

After signing the treaty where he was camped, on the plain of Hudaybiyah, Muhammad's camp buzzed with resentment. They had marched four days to visit the Holy House and make sacrifice. Why should they turn back when they were in sight of the city walls?

Umar, one of the angriest, stood up and challenged Muhammad to his face. "Are you not the prophet of God? Isn't our cause right and the Quraysh's wrong? Haven't you promised us that we would make seven circles around the Kaaba?"

Meekly Muhammad nodded yes to each question, but when Umar got to the last, he replied, "I promised you worship at the Kaaba, but did I say it would be this year?"

A tricky answer, but Umar sat down, and there was no rebellion. Still, Muhammad needed a revelation. And one came. God told him that certain victory (Al-Fath) had been won. Therefore, Muhammad ordered that the sacrificial animals be sacrificed outside the city walls. He strode outside and made the first sacrifice of a prize camel. Some of his followers grumbled, but when he appeared before them to have his head shaved, as a sign that the holy rites had been successful, they complied. Their shorn hair was carried by the wind to the gates of Mecca. It slipped under and littered the holy sites themselves. The Prophet knew what he was about.

As I feared, the treaty was thin. A few night raids on one side, a few murders on the other. Arabs suckle on strife, and they are never weaned. What the desert makes us suffer, we make our enemies suffer. But I had lost the will to fight back. I became a negotiator hoping to extract a few bits of privilege, a little more breathing room before the final blow came.

We had turned the Muslims away the first time they came to worship, but the second time, a year later, couldn't be finessed. I sent word that Muhammad and his followers could enter Mecca, but only after all the Quraysh had abandoned the city. We would sit up in the hills for three days and wait out their visit. This was offered as a gesture of peace, to ensure that the pilgrims wouldn't run into violence. Muhammad knew that it was a mark of disdain as well.

Muhammad entered the gates of an abandoned city and drew within sight of the Kaaba. Walking up to it, he silently touched the Black Stone with his staff and gave thanks to Allah. The company of worshipers was deeply moved, thinking how many years it had been since he could do that. When Muhammad approached the door, however, it was locked. My doing, I'll admit it. I was damned if he would defile the inner sanctum. His followers grew enraged. I imagine they would have torn the city apart. Looking down from the hilltop, I half expected to see Mecca engulfed in smoke. Remaining calm, Muhammad ordered Bilal, a former slave, to climb to the roof of the Holy House and call the faithful to their noon prayers. When Mecca heard a Muslim singing out over the rooftops, the followers were satisfied.

My disdain was pointless, anyway. The new faith spread like a fever into every household. You couldn't see it, yet it overcame you even as you breathed. My own daughter, Ramlah, was lost to me. I renounced her when she ran off with a Muslim on the Hijra. One day soon after that I found my wife weeping.

"What is it?" I asked.

"There is no more Ramlah. She is now Umm Abibah."

I shook my head. "Her husband died. He was a dolt and a traitor. And now she has a right to be a wife again."

"You think so? Well you have your wish. She is now the wife of Muhammad."

All the blood drained from my face, and I staggered to a chair. For the rest of the day and all that night I remained there, as if paralyzed. Nursing my grievances, my mind drifted back in time when I could walk past Muhammad in the street and not bestow a glance. But I'm a realist. The thin treaty turned worthless. I was sent to Medina in the hopes of fooling Muhammad into signing it again. No one was fooled. All the power was on his side now.

Maybe I was lonely in Medina. Something caused me to make a mistake. I went to my daughter, in the rooms she kept near Muhammad. What good did I think would come of it? She was nervous and stiff, barely bending to the floor to greet me. I saw a chair and began to sit down.

"Oh no!" she said timidly, snatching off the blanket that covered it.

I kept my temper. "You would deny respect to your father? It's only a wool blanket, not embroidered silk from Cathay."

"But the Prophet sits on it," she stammered. I stared at her, then turned on my heels and left without a word.

It has been told that it took three years before Muhammad swallowed Mecca. In the end, the city fell without resistance. Before the Muslims marched in, they sent a declaration ahead of them. Any citizen who stayed in his house behind locked doors would be spared. So that's what we did. I cowered by lamplight as the horses of the Muslims clanged their iron hoofs on the cobblestones. I didn't trust these warriors for God completely. I ordered that the lamps be kept low, so that the invaders would think my house was empty. All I could see in the darkness was the glint of fear in my wife's eyes. I never asked what she saw in mine.

There was no avoiding my fate. I had to face him.

"I will convert," I said, offering no conditions. I licked my lips, preparing to kiss his sandals, but Muhammad stopped me with a small gesture.

"You only need to swear two things. The first is that there is no god but God."

I repeated the words. If you have lived as long as I have, your allegiance is greasy. It shifts easily from one god to the next.

"And the second thing?" I asked.

"There is no God but God, and Muhammad is His prophet."

The words fell simply from his lips. He didn't puff himself up like an emperor. I knew that his struggles had humbled him. He had an infant son, Ibrahim, born in Medina. Muhammad doted on the babe, but one day he caught a fever and died. Then he sent a band of his best warriors to Syria, but they were ambushed by mercenaries from Byzantium. His foster son, Zayd, was killed, and with him a cousin, Jafar. Both were precious to Muhammad. An ordinary man wouldn't love his God quite so dearly after that. Or trust him.

One of the companions standing behind Muhammad cleared his throat. "There is no God but God, and Muhammad is His prophet."

I suppose he was coaxing me. If I didn't repeat the words, who knows what would come next? For all his mercy, I had fought Muhammad bitterly in one campaign after the next.

Holding my feelings in, I rose to my feet. "Give me time to think."

I strode out of his tent without looking back. For all I knew, a dagger could have plunged into my skull.

Few here in Mecca remember old Muttalib, the Prophet's grandfather. If they do, it's because he used to dote on his grandson, bouncing him on his knee while we drank and argued at the inns around the Kaaba. But I remember something else.

I returned to Muhammad's tent the next day.

"You've made up your mind," he said. "I won't ask. You wouldn't be here if you weren't ready to submit." He saw how I faintly cringed. "You aren't submitting to me."

I had wasted enough time. I knelt before Muhammad and proclaimed, "There is no God but God, and Muhammad is His prophet."

Muhammad gave a faint nod, satisfied, and I rose to my feet.

I could have walked out, but instead I asked, "When is God's love so intense that it feels like hate?"

"My grandfather, Muttalib, used to ask that question," said Muhammad soberly.

"I know. I heard him. I was almost a man when you sat on his knee. But no matter. Your grandfather planted a seed. That's undeniable. He worried about his soul while the rest of us were only worrying about money and women. You have the same strangeness about you. No wonder."

Muhammad nodded. "And I still ask the same question. You aren't my brother, not yet. Allah means nothing to you. I imagine you're the one who tried to humiliate me at the Kaaba."

"Perhaps."

He died two years later, at the age of sixty-two. There was no great crisis, just a steady withering. He lost his strength the way a great tree loses sap. His

last moments, they say, were spent with his head rest-
ing in the lap of his favorite wife, Aisha. The end was
gentle; the faithful were certain that the Prophet would
be waiting for them in Paradise, where the trees are
greener than any in Arabia, the virgins more beautiful,
the crystal rivers sparkling under the sun.

Even in death, Arabia is his. Syria and Egypt
will fall soon. The emperor of Persia trembles when
the Prophet's emissaries appear before his throne.
Muhammad was told by God to send letters to all the
rulers of the earth, informing them that they must
heed the Lord's word and convert. Without hesitation
he sent the letters. Imagine.

The Prophet died in Medina, and it was deemed best
to bury him there, in the courtyard of the house where
he had lived. I watched the funeral without rancor.
Beside me was Abu Bakr. Tribe and trade once united
us, before we became sworn enemies. Now he is calmly
accepting of my conversion. We are tied by faith, and
Abu Bakr makes that a cause for smiles. In the confusion after Muhammad's death, several companions had
a claim to his leadership. Ali had been chosen years ago,
but he was a boy then. Umar and Uthman led strong
factions. I imagine their heads swam at the prospect of
ruling the world that Allah had handed them. But in
the end it was Abu Bakr whom the chiefs chose. They

call him *caliph*, successor to the Prophet's authority in heaven and on earth. A good choice. Abu Bakr is loved by everyone. One of his most lovable qualities is his age. The old man won't sit on the throne for long. The young rivals still have hope.

I move among them freely, a prize convert and a harmless dog with its teeth pulled. My end is near. My wife is sick, soon to leave me. She is half blind already. She can't see me when I sit by the lamp and read the Koran. What would she do if she could see that? My eyes fall on words that God must have sent especially to old men:

Every soul will meet death.
You will find your true reward only on the Day of
    Resurrection.
This world is nothing but illusory pleasure.

I have known illusion and pleasure, and both to the fullest. Is that my real bond with the Prophet?

When I laid my wife in the earth, Aisha came to see me. She married so young, as a mere child, that she still looks beautiful. She entered my house looking stately, and for a moment her eyes and the pearls she wore around her neck made the dim room shuttered against the sun seem bright.

"You will meet her again in Paradise," Aisha murmured, taking my hand. It trembled slightly in hers. I couldn't tell if it was from grief or age. Both, no doubt.

"My wife didn't convert," I said. "Doesn't that mean she is lost?"

"Love will draw her to you. That will be her way to God."

It was a comforting lie, and I was glad to hear it. Aisha sat with me for a while. The sunlight that seeped through the shutters glanced off her necklace, turning it into glistening tears.

"I want you to believe something," she said. She saw me stiffen. "I didn't come to preach. This is a story, the one I hold closest to my heart. On a cool night in Mecca the Prophet was walking to his house when he suddenly was overcome with sleep. He lay down in a doorway near the Kaaba. The next thing he knew, the angel Gabriel appeared and sent his light into the Prophet's chest. The intensity of the feeling sharpened every sense, and the Prophet realized that his heart was being purified for something wondrous. Gabriel pointed to the end of the street where a winged beast stood. It was white and shaped like a donkey, yet larger. Calling the creature Buraq, the angel bade the Prophet to mount it. The instant he did, he discovered that Buraq was a lightning steed. Each of its steps reached as far as the horizon.

The Prophet was struck with awe and fear. In a matter of minutes they made a journey as far as the farthest mosque, which stood in Jerusalem. At that time there was no mosque there, but Gabriel assured the Prophet of their destination. Inside the mosque were many holy fathers and prophets who had come before. After praying with them, the Prophet was told to remount Buraq, for his night journey was only half begun."

Aisha's voice rose and fell in the dark. Her eyes sparkled in the near darkness. Among the Arabs, no one is more esteemed than a poet. I never knew of a woman poet, but she could have been one. I felt myself filled with the scent of roses.

"When the Prophet got back on Buraq, he looked to the horizon, where the next step would land them. Instead, with a clanging hoofbeat that printed the rock beneath its feet, the creature soared into the sky. The stars came as near as a bonfire in the Prophet's courtyard. They passed through the crystal dome of the sky, higher and higher. How could this be? He was still alive, yet the Prophet was entering the seven heavens. Each was dazzling to the eyes and blissful to the heart. When they reached the seventh heaven, a tree blocked the way. This was the sacred tree that no angel could set foot beyond. And yet the Prophet was allowed to enter. He exchanged holy words with the great forebears of Islam, first Abraham, then Moses, and finally Jesus. The final gift was to be ushered into the presence of Allah. Before the Most Glorious the Prophet was reduced to awed silence. Allah spoke and gave him guidance for the faithful. Their first duty, said God, was to pray fifty times a day. The Prophet bowed in obedience and withdrew. When he was back among the elder prophets, Moses asked him what God had said. When he heard about the duty to pray fifty times a day, Moses shook his head. 'That is impossible. Go back and ask for an easier way.' The Prophet returned to Allah not once but several times, until his pleas were heard. God granted that the faithful should pray not fifty, but five times a day."

In the dark Aisha heard me chuckle. She stopped telling me her tale.

"Don't be angry," I said. "You've brought me a smile. I always knew the Prophet was canny. He even talked God around to his way."

I couldn't see Aisha's reaction, but she didn't scold me. Maybe she smiled, too. But the story came to an abrupt end. The lightning steed brought Muhammad back to earth, and he woke up shivering in the night air where he had fallen asleep.

"Was it a dream?" I asked.

"Many thought so, even those among the companions. They were shaken. The Prophet had received revelations, but he always insisted he was a man among men, not a miracle worker. One of them rushed to tell the story to my father, Abu Bakr."

"Ah," I said. In those days I shunned Abu Bakr and barely recalled that he was Aisha's father. "And he believed?"

"Without hesitation. He said, 'If Muhammad tells us that his journey wasn't a dream, I have no choice but to believe him. Don't I already accept that the angel comes to him?' It was from my father that I heard the story."

I felt Aisha's hand press into mine again. "But you began by saying that you live this story," I said.

"Every day. I take a journey to heaven, you see. That's the treasure the Prophet gave us all. He opened the way so that we can follow him. We don't need Buraq to reach God. Our steed is the soul."

Forgive me, but I was overcome. It was too much. My wife was gone. My body would lie next to hers very soon. What was left to me but a journey to heaven, if that's possible? I held Aisha's hand with a tight grip. Tears ran down my cheeks and were caught in the deep wrinkles there.

"*Allahu Akbar*," I whispered. "God is great."

"*Allahu Akbar*," she repeated and slipped from the room, leaving behind the glimmer of pearls and the faint scent of roses.

Afterword
A Walk with Muhammad

F ew can read the life of Muhammad without feeling excited and disturbed at the same time. I
think he must have had the same conflicting reactions
himself. Islam was born in a cradle of turmoil, and the
arrival of Allah, one God who vanquished hundreds
of ancient Arabian gods, caused an upheaval. A single
individual had to carry the burden of violence with the
awe of revelation.

Muhammad didn't see himself like Jesus, called the
Son of God, or like Buddha, a prince who achieved
sublime, cosmic enlightenment. An Indian proverb
holds that it only takes a spark to burn down the whole
forest. Muhammad struck that spark.

If the Prophet's life were a fairy tale, he would march
down from his mountain cave, spread his arms like a

latter-day Moses, and tell the people what God wanted them to do. In real life, Muhammad reacted with fear and trembling. You and I would also fear madness if the angel Gabriel appeared in a flash of blinding light and told us that our mission was to redeem the sinful world.

God did not leave Muhammad alone. When a revelation was at hand, Muhammad went into a trance state that deprived him of his own will. His face became flushed; he sweated profusely. The messages he received were dire. The fate of the Arabs depended on him. Muhammad's divine task was to convince his people to renounce their ancestral idol worship and superstitious veneration of multiple gods. If they didn't, Allah had apocalyptic punishment in mind. No sinner would be forgiven. Only those who feared God and obeyed him to the letter would be saved. As for the Prophet himself, his freedom of choice was steadily removed, until the only path left was the proverbial razor's edge: every word, act, and thought was surrendered to God.

A more fearful destiny is hard to imagine. Muhammad said, on various occasions and in various ways, "The best in life comes from Allah. The worst is my fault." He took that attitude, giving all the praise to God and taking all the blame on himself. Not that every moment was about life and death. God had a way of solving Muhammad's everyday problems. One of his favorite wives, Aisha, stopped at an oasis by herself one day. A dashing Muslim rider came by and offered to escort her on her journey. They were alone together for a night, and tongues began to wag. Eventually petty gossip turned into a major scandal. The Prophet prayed to Allah, and a revelation came. Aisha was innocent. Anyone who spoke out against her was to be whipped.

In the same vein, Muhammad had helpful revelations that his various wives should stop bickering among themselves. God told the women around him to obey their husband in all things. The Almighty sometimes mentioned the Prophet's enemies by name in the Koran and roundly condemned them. He offered hints about how to debate with critics and naysayers. When the Muslim exiles tried to reenter Mecca and were turned back, there was a revelation to tell them that their apparent defeat was really a victory.

Muhammad could count upon God's counsel to extricate him from almost any tight place. Scholars divide the revelations, amounting to thousands of separate messages, into two main parts. The ones that came in Mecca focus on theology; the messages that came in Medina, after the Hijra, or migration, of 622 CE, mostly center on managing the new faith and the newly faithful.

The Koran is about salvation and apocalypse—just as in Jesus's lifetime, the early converts to Islam believed that the end of the world was at hand. But the Koran is also about war, politics, infighting, treaties, jealousies, and the everyday headaches of running the government in Medina, including the collection of taxes.

PRACTICAL REDEMPTION

All religions attempt to bring worshipers closer to God, but few are as explicit as the Koran. The famous "five pillars of Islam" prescribe the duties of the faithful:

The profession of faith, declaring that Allah is the one God and Muhammad his prophet.

Prayer, which takes place five times a day facing Mecca, the most sacred place on earth.

Charity, through the giving of alms to the poor.

Fasting during the month of Ramadan.

Pilgrimage, at least once in a lifetime, to Mecca.

Each of these duties is a reminder that earthly life exists for one purpose: to redeem fallen humanity. One can see a common thread in the five pillars: by prayer, professing one's faith, or taking a month off to turn inward, the worshiper sets ordinary affairs aside, allowing space for God to enter. Redemption is turned into a practical matter of things to do, and you can look out your window to see how your neighbors are coming along, as they can with you. This became deeply important when the first Muslims had to defend themselves from persecution by drawing into a tight community of believers, the Ummah. The image of presenting a united front against a hostile world remains potent today.

The tight bonding of believers didn't leave out theology. There are six core beliefs that would be agreed upon even by sects that otherwise divide along fierce lines like the Sunni and Shia. These beliefs are:

Belief in Allah as the only true God

Belief in the prophets sent by God as well as lesser messengers and warners

Belief in angels

Belief in the books sent by God: the Torah, the Gospels, and the Koran

Belief in judgment day and the resurrection of the dead

Belief in fate, whether good or bad

These beliefs overlap closely with those of both Judaism and Christianity. But no religion can escape the claim that it surmounts all others. This is also true with Islam, which sees itself as "confirming" the past, meaning that God updated his old message as written in the Torah and the New Testament. He sent a new prophet whose word was final; therefore Jews and Christians should pay attention and convert. This would show their true belief in the one God. Naturally, there was much resistance to this idea, and the result has been a long, sad history of religious conflict.

Allah wanted the updated message to be complete. As a result, Islam became more than a religion; it is a way of life so all-consuming that nothing has been left to chance. God has a commandment for everything. In case there are any gaps, thousands of *hadith* exist to guide the course of everybody's daily affairs. A *hadith* is a story or incident in the Prophet's life. It indicates how he reacted when somebody brought a problem to him or a lawsuit or a question about right and wrong. Aisha, the favored wife whom Muhammad married when she was a small child, long outlived him. She became the source of some two thousand *hadith*. These have the force of law, even today. So while Christians may muse over "What would Jesus do?" the parallel question has a literal answer for Muslims. There are few crises in life, major or minor, where the faithful don't know exactly what Muhammad would do.

One should note that a great deal of Islamic doctrine evolved after the Prophet's death, which came suddenly. Jesus's disciples were also suddenly bereft after the crucifixion. Muhammad's followers were disconcerted, but quickly began to assemble a complete, authorized Koran from all the existing suras. The compilation went through struggles and arguments, needless to say, leaving enough disputes to occupy generations of scholars and interpreters.

THE PATH OF SUBMISSION

Because the Prophet's life was filled with God's instructions, almost by the minute, for today's Muslims the path to leading a good life leaves no room for doubt. The highest virtue in Islam is surrender or submission. Those of us standing outside the faith may have a difficult time understanding this virtue. We reject the absence of free choice. Most of us want to have it both ways, to obey God some of the time and make up our own minds the rest of the time. Islam, to be blunt, considers that the path to damnation. Why would anyone willingly set his or her own sinful desires against the precious word of God? Why would a person choose to live a single moment apart from the divine?

There's no getting around this vital difference, and it explains many things. For one, it explains the spread of Islam, which happened like wildfire within a few years of Muhammad's death. His companions, the handful who migrated to Medina with him, began life as merchants and traders in Mecca. But Ali, Umar, and Uthman ended their lives as caliphs, rulers of an empire that extended from Egypt to Persia. This vast expansion wasn't due to warfare, although the Muslims were fierce warriors. Instead, Islam offered closeness to God. Closeness to God is a human yearning that wants to be fulfilled. Islam didn't fulfill it in theory, but in everyday actions.

Ordinary people were used to praying to idols and offering sacrifices in return for rewards as basic as a good crop and a reliable water supply. Allah took over the functions of hundreds of idols, and in addition there was the promise of going to Paradise after death, dwelling forever in the Garden.

If the promise is delightful, the reverse is terrifying. Living according to your own whims, without regard for God's commands, leads to hellfire. That is why modernism has met with stubborn resistance in the Islamic world. Going on the Internet, watching television, or attending a nightclub could imperil your soul. Orthodoxy is always that way, regardless of the faith. Muslims don't hold a patent on fearing the creeping infection of secularism. Fundamentalists in every faith hold the same suspicions. To them, the worldly has always been the enemy of the other-worldly.

If we look at Arabia before Muhammad, life was so harsh that it must have come as an immense relief to find a way that promised not just eternal life, but things far more basic: the end of blood feuds, a sense of belonging, the comfort of one faith for one people, and simple rules for getting along. The life dictated by the Koran wasn't a prison deprived of free will—it was order in place of chaos.

The tale of Muhammad and the five mares is central here. As recounted in the novel, Muhammad had a string of horses that he loved. It was his habit to take them out into the desert for a run. One day he took them out so far from Medina that the animals became desperately thirsty. Up ahead they smelled an oasis and began to gallop toward it. Muhammad let them reach almost to the water hole, and then he gave a sharp whistle for them to return. Most of the horses kept running, but five mares turned around and returned to the Prophet's hand. He used these five mares to breed the strain of Arabian horses that are most prized today.

The story is a parable about religious obedience, and when it's told, the moral is that God favors loyalty above all other virtues.

THE RETURN OF THE LOST

One has to remember that the Arabs of Muhammad's time felt like a people who had been left behind. The desert isolated them almost completely, making them safe from invasion, but also immune to religious influence. I was amazed to read that during Muhammad's childhood not a single Bible could have been found in the Arabian Peninsula. The dominant tribe in Mecca, the Quraysh, considered themselves the children of Abraham. And yet they also knew that Abraham's religion had been lost; they inherited only scraps and dusty remains. That's why the myth of Zamzam, the well that God created to bring water to his children, was so crucial. When Zamzam was lost, so was the water of life. When it was found again, by the Qurayshi chieftain Muttalib, the water of life returned.

Muhammad was in the direct line of Muttalib, who was his grandfather. History writes itself from front to back, and once Islam thrived, writers were quick to revisit the Prophet's early life and fill it with portents and omens. They had Christ in mind as a rough model. We are given a lone mystical hermit who lays hands on the head of the boy Muhammad and predicts that he will be the prophet foretold by the Bible. In Medina another mystic, a Jewish rabbi, arrives to proclaim that the last prophet is at hand. In Mecca a handful of monotheists, known as *hanif,* instruct the young orphan in their ways, and the most outspoken of them, Waraqah, is bold enough to proclaim Muhammad as the chosen one at the very doors of the Kaaba.

If this is exciting, the disturbing parts aren't far behind. The Jews of Medina were the first to welcome Muhammad and his tiny band of followers into their midst. The young faith was quite fragile. No more than a dozen close followers, the companions, had developed over the twelve years since the first revelation. For the first three years Muhammad told no one about his calling outside his family. Under constant threats from the Quraysh, perhaps forty to a hundred converts emerged before the Hijra. It is remarkable that the Jews of Medina were willing to accept Muhammad as someone to judge their disputes and to draw up a plan for bringing peace to all the warring tribes in the city.

Yet in the next few years, as the faithful grew in numbers, God told Muhammad to drive the Jewish tribes out of Medina, exiling them to marginal wastelands. Later, when Jewish resentment flared up and the last remaining tribe cooperated with the invading army from Mecca, Muhammad exercised violent retribution. All the men were beheaded, and the women and children divided as the spoils of war, many to be sold into slavery. This horrifying decision, because it came by revelation, has been praised by Islamic historians. Only in recent times have some revisionists considered it as the barbaric crime it is.

Here we meet the dark underside of the Prophet's mission. His every act and word has the force of God behind it (except perhaps only the "satanic verses" in the Koran, so called because they were inspired by demonic forces to delude and briefly mislead Muhammad—he soon saw through them and returned to Allah's guidance). I don't think Muhammad believed himself to be infallible. We have touching stories about his humility. He admitted his mistakes, and far from being the only one to give orders in times of crisis, he sat in council with his chieftains and listened to their voices.

After his death, the ranks closed around absolute truth, which meant that it was a test of faith to turn any act by the Prophet, even the beheading of his enemies, into something right and good. On this point, the critics of Muhammad cite his marriage to Aisha. She was the youngest daughter of Abu Bakr, the merchant who stood up among the first and most devout of the new Muslims. At the age of six Aisha was betrothed to a husband, until Muhammad had a revelation that she was meant for him. The prospective groom was persuaded to give her up. The marriage to Muhammad took place but wasn't consummated until Aisha was nine. Beyond Islam, this episode is more than distasteful. Within the faith, however, it is praised. None of Muhammad's other wives were virgins, and the rationale is that Aisha served as a kind of Virgin Mary, made all the more pure because she was so young. To the outside world, this is a prescription for blind fanaticism.

CLOSING THE GAP

The bald fact is that we cannot identify with customs that exist across such a yawning abyss. And as mentioned, every faith closes ranks around its own version of the absolute truth. Islamic extremism is no exception, and unfortunately the loud minority have poisoned our view.

The God who speaks in the Koran isn't simply an Old Testament God with revenge and punishment in mind, whimsically deciding who will be rewarded or destroyed. The Koran affirms Judaism and Christianity. The most significant mystical event in Muhammad's life was the night journey he took to Jerusalem on the back of a lightning steed. Muhammad worshiped there with his predecessors and then was lifted up to the seventh heaven, where he communed with Abraham, Moses, and Jesus before being ushered into the presence of Allah.

The purpose of the Koran, to borrow Jesus's words, was to fulfill the law, not to break it. It took warfare to spread the new faith, but just over the horizon was a Paradise in which one God welcomed all believers. We can say that Islam brought monotheism to replace polytheism—the Arabs got one God in place of many. But the message was more universal. Allah wasn't Yahweh dressed in a caftan. He was the One, an all-pervasive presence that upheld the cosmos.

Every Muslim loves the Prophet, but one special branch of Islam developed an intense, mystical love for Allah—the Sufis. Within their approach to God, we can glimpse the immense beauty and power of Muhammad's legacy. In my childhood, I was taken to visit Sufi shrines, usually the graves of saints who were prayed to for miracles. There were all-night poetry readings and dancing, truly ecstatic events. For me, these Sufis, with their extreme courtesy to one another and the ever present reminder of God's love, stood for

Islam—white domes against the sky, romantic tales of princes and princesses, and the hypnotic call of the muezzins from their minarets.

The sweetness of these images is real, even if history has added a bitter aftertaste. Sufis strove for unity with God, and their path to enlightenment was love. Devotion led to rapture, and rapture led to the Infinite. No romance of the soul is more extreme, as witnessed in this poem by Rumi, the greatest Sufi mystic:

You miracle-seekers are always looking for signs,
You go to bed crying and wake up in tears.
You plead for what doesn't come
Until it darkens your days.
You sacrifice everything, even your mind,
You sit down in the fire, wanting to become ashes,
And when you meet with a sword,
You throw yourself on it.
Fall into the habit of such helpless mad things—
You will have your sign.

These lines aren't a flight of fancy—they describe what Sufis actually did to reach God. The beauty of union with the One was exquisite, but the seeker burned himself to ashes before reaching his Beloved.

If Muhammad opened the door to God, Sufis were the ones who flung themselves through it, blindly and crying out with passion. This ardent striving is the best interpretation of *jihad*, and the one I hope will prevail. It brings light out of darkness, as Rumi proclaimed:

In love that is new—there must you die.
Where the path begins on the other side.
Melt into the sky and break free
From the prison whose walls you must smash.
Greet the hue of day
Out of a fog of darkness.
Now is the time!

Muhammad's ultimate legacy was to make time for the timeless. The One has no limitations in time and space. No face or body can be assigned to Him, which is why Islam forbids portrayals of God. By comparison to Allah's transcendent reality, the world below is a trifling illusion. Thus the heart of Islam calls the faithful to look beyond illusion to find reality. For the Sufis, fear of a punishing Father evolved into a love affair with the invisible One, whose essence is mercy, compassion, and the sacredness of all life.

Muhammad can be judged by the worst of his followers or the best. He can be blamed for planting the seeds of fanaticism and *jihad* or praised for bringing the word of God to a wasteland. In my walk with Muhammad I found that every preconception was unfair. What the Prophet bequeathed to the world is entangled with the best and worst in all of us.

I doubt that the angel Gabriel has an appointment to meet me in a flash of blinding light. But if he does, I'd expect to wrestle with revelation every day. God didn't make life easier for Muhammad. He made it far more difficult, and the wonder of his story is how he brought light out of darkness with all the fallibility of "a man among men." The message he brought wasn't pure; it never is. As long as our yearning for God exceeds our ability to live in holiness, the tangled mystery of the Prophet will be our own mystery too.